Living in the IT Era

Introduction to Basic Computing

Paul Omar P. Gangoso

Table of Contents

Chapter 1: What is Information Technology? 7

    IT Defined 8

    Evolution of Information Technology 14

        IT and the Industrial Revolution 17

        IT and the Fourth Industrial Revolution 19

    IT vs ICT 21

    IT in our Daily life 23

    Activity Guide 26

Chapter 2: What is a Computer? 27

    How does a Computer Work? 28

    Classifications 34

    Evolution of Computers 38

    Computer Hardwares 52

    What is System Software? 56

    System Functions 62

    OS Functions 63

        Resource Management 65

        Process Management 66

        Memory Management 68

        CPU Management 70

        Storage Management 71

        Device Management 77

    Types of OS 78

    Application Systems 84

    System Utilities 93

        Productivity Softwares 95

Communication Software 97

Multimedia Software 98

Utility Software 100

Gaming Software 100

Software Development 103

Cloud Computing and AI 107

Cloud Computing 108

Artificial Intelligence (AI) 109

Discussion Guide 112

Activity Guide 112

Chapter 3: The Internet 115

The Internet Defined 116

How does the Internet Work? 117

What is an IP Address? 119

What is a Website? 120

What is DNS? 123

What is a Domain Name? 126

Email 129

Web Browsers 133

Search Engines 134

The Social Media 138

Social Media Uses 141

Pro's and Con's 145

IoT 149

Discussion Guide 150

Activity Guide 151

Chapter 4: Data Security and Privacy 153

What is Data Security?.. 154

    Definition 154

    Data Security Breach 154

Hacking 156

Malware 161

Phishing.. 163

Physical Theft 167

Insider Threats 169

    Reflection / Example... 171

The Philippine Data Privacy Act 172

Data Security and Privacy in Social Media 174

    Steps in Preventing Personal Data Risks in using Social Media. 176

Cyberbullying 179

Cyberlibel 183

Discussion Guide.. 184

Activity Guide.. 184

Bibliography.. 186

Chapter 1: What is Information Technology?

IT Defined

Information Technology (IT) refers to the use of computer systems, software, and networks to process, store, and transmit data and information. IT is a broad field that encompasses various technologies and applications, including hardware, software, telecommunications, and databases.

IT professionals are responsible for designing, developing, and maintaining computer systems and networks to meet the needs of individuals and organizations. They work in various industries, including healthcare, finance, education, and government.

Information technology is extremely important to people in today's world for the following reasons:

1. Communication: Information technology has revolutionized the way people communicate, making it faster, easier, and more convenient. People can communicate with each other from anywhere in the world through email, instant messaging, video conferencing, and social media.

2. Education: Information technology has transformed education by making it more accessible and interactive. Online courses, e-books,

and educational software have made learning more flexible and convenient.

3. Business: Information technology has transformed the way businesses operate, making them more efficient and productive. Businesses can now use technology to automate processes, manage data, and communicate with customers and suppliers.

4. Healthcare: Information technology has improved healthcare by making it easier to access medical records, share information between healthcare providers, and monitor patients remotely.

5. Entertainment: Information technology has transformed the entertainment industry, providing people with access to a wide range of content, including movies, music, and games.

6. Society: Information technology has had a significant impact on society, enabling people to connect with each other, access information, and participate in social and political activities.

Information Technology is categorized according to areas of functions. These are:

1. Computer hardware: This includes the physical components of a computer system, such as the central processing unit (CPU), memory, storage devices, and input/output devices.

2. Software development: This includes the creation of software applications, such as operating systems, productivity software, and games.

3. Networking: This includes the design and maintenance of computer networks, including local area networks (LANs) and wide area networks (WANs).

4. Cybersecurity: This includes the protection of computer systems and networks from unauthorized access, theft, and damage.

5. Database management: This includes the design, development, and maintenance of databases that store and organize data.

To say that we are living in the IT era means that we are currently in a time period where information technology (IT) plays a central role in various aspects of our lives. IT encompasses the use of computers, software, networks, and electronic systems to store, process, transmit, and retrieve information. Living in the IT era further means that technology has permeated various aspects of our lives, transforming the way we work, communicate, access information, and solve problems. It has opened up new opportunities, improved efficiency, and connected people globally.

Technological Advancements

We are witnessing rapid advancements in technology, such as the development of faster computers, more powerful software, and more efficient communication systems. This has led to increased accessibility and availability of IT resources.

Global Connectivity

The internet has connected people from all around the world, enabling instant communication and sharing of information. It has transformed various sectors, including business, education, healthcare, and entertainment, by allowing for remote collaboration, e-commerce, online learning platforms, telemedicine, and digital entertainment streaming.

Digitization of Information

Information is no longer limited to physical forms like books or documents. With the widespread use of digital devices, information is increasingly being digitized and stored in electronic formats, making it more easily accessible, searchable, and shareable.

Automation and Artificial Intelligence (AI)

The IT era has witnessed significant developments in automation and AI technologies. These advancements have led to the automation of various processes, increased efficiency, and the ability to analyze and make sense of large amounts of data. AI is being leveraged in various sectors like healthcare, finance, transportation, and manufacturing to optimize operations and improve decision-making.

Mobile and Cloud Computing

The rise of mobile devices, such as smartphones and tablets, has transformed the way we access and interact with information. Cloud computing has also gained prominence, allowing for the storage and processing of data on remote servers, providing users with seamless access to their data from anywhere and at any time.

Data-centric Approaches

Data has become a valuable resource in the IT era. Organizations and individuals are collecting, analyzing, and utilizing data to gain insights, make informed decisions, and enhance processes and services. Big data analytics and data-driven decision-making have become a significant focus.

Cybersecurity Challenges

With increased reliance on IT, there is a growing need for robust cybersecurity measures to protect sensitive information from cyber threats. The IT era has seen an upsurge in cybercrimes, leading to an increased emphasis on cybersecurity awareness, practices, and technologies. Cybersecurity challenges refer to the issues and concerns faced in protecting computer systems, networks, and data from unauthorized access, attacks, and theft. Some key challenges in cybersecurity include: Increasing sophistication of cyber threats, Insider threats, Lack of awareness and training, Rapidly evolving technology, Third-party risks, Lack of skilled cybersecurity professionals, Compliance with regulations, : Complexity of networks and systems, Advanced persistent threats (APTs), and Privacy concerns.

Evolution of Information Technology

The evolution of information technology can be traced back to the early 1800s with the development of the first mechanical calculator by Charles Babbage. Since then, the field has undergone significant advancements and innovations. Here are some key milestones in the evolution of information technology:

1. The invention of the telegraph in the mid-1800s allowed for long-distance communication for the first time.

2. The development of the first computers in the mid-1900s, such as the ENIAC and UNIVAC, marked the beginning of the digital age.

3. The introduction of the first programming languages, such as FORTRAN and COBOL, in the 1950s and 1960s made it easier to program computers.

4. The development of the first microprocessors in the early 1970s made it possible to create smaller and more powerful computers.

5. The invention of the personal computer in the late 1970s and early 1980s made computing accessible to individuals and small businesses.

6. The development of the internet in the 1990s revolutionized communication and information sharing.

7. The introduction of smartphones in the early 2000s allowed people to access the internet and communicate on-the-go.

8. The rise of cloud computing in the 2010s made it possible to store and access data and applications remotely.

9. The development of artificial intelligence and machine learning in recent years has opened up new possibilities for automation and data analysis.

The advancement of information technology has been rapid and transformative, with new technologies and innovations emerging at an unprecedented pace. Here are some key areas of advancement in information technology:

1. Artificial intelligence (AI): AI has advanced significantly in recent years, enabling machines to perform tasks that were previously only possible for humans. AI is used in a wide range of applications, including natural language processing, computer vision, and robotics.

2. Big data: The amount of data being generated and collected has grown exponentially in recent years, leading to the development of big data technologies that can store, process, and analyze large amounts of data.

3. Cloud computing: Cloud computing has revolutionized the way businesses and individuals access and use computing resources. Cloud computing allows users to access data and applications remotely, making it easier to collaborate and work from anywhere.

4. Internet of Things (IoT): IoT refers to the network of physical devices, vehicles, and other objects that are embedded with sensors, software, and connectivity, allowing them to collect and exchange data. IoT has enabled new applications in areas such as smart homes, healthcare, and transportation.

5. Blockchain: Blockchain is a distributed ledger technology that enables secure and transparent transactions without the need for intermediaries. Blockchain has the potential to transform industries such as finance, supply chain management, and healthcare.

6. Virtual and augmented reality: Virtual and augmented reality technologies have advanced significantly in recent years, enabling immersive experiences in gaming, entertainment, education, and other areas.

In brief, the advancement of information technology has had a profound impact on society, transforming the way we work, communicate, and live. As technology continues to advance, it is likely to have an even greater impact on our lives in the future.

IT and the Industrial Revolution

Information technology has had a significant impact on the industrial revolution. The industrial revolution was a period of significant change in the late 18th and early 19th centuries, characterized by the introduction of new manufacturing processes, machinery, and technologies. Here are some ways in which information technology has impacted the industrial revolution:

1. Automation: Information technology has enabled automation of many industrial processes, reducing the need for human labor and increasing efficiency. This has led to increased productivity and lower costs.

2. Data Analysis: Information technology has enabled the collection and analysis of data from various sources, allowing companies to make informed decisions about their operations. This has led to improved efficiency and reduced waste.

3. Supply Chain Management: Information technology has enabled better management of the supply chain, allowing companies to track inventory, manage logistics, and optimize production schedules. This has led to reduced costs and improved customer satisfaction.

4. Communication: Information technology has enabled better communication between different parts of the organization, as well as between different organizations in the supply chain. This has led to improved collaboration and coordination, reducing delays and improving overall efficiency.

5. Innovation: Information technology has enabled the development of new products and services, as well as new manufacturing processes. This has led to increased competition and innovation, driving the industrial revolution forward.

In summary, information technology has played a significant role in the industrial revolution, enabling companies to improve their operations and compete more effectively in the global marketplace.

IT and the Fourth Industrial Revolution

Information technology is a key driver of the fourth industrial revolution, also known as Industry 4.0. The fourth industrial revolution is characterized by the integration of advanced technologies such as artificial intelligence, the Internet of Things (IoT), robotics, and big data analytics, into manufacturing and other industries. Here are some ways in which information technology creates the fourth industrial revolution:

1. Connectivity: Information technology enables the connectivity of machines, devices, and systems, creating a network of interconnected devices that can communicate with each other and share data. This connectivity enables the automation of processes and the optimization of production.

2. Big Data Analytics: Information technology enables the collection, storage, and analysis of large amounts of data, allowing companies to gain insights into their operations and make informed decisions. Big data analytics can help companies optimize production, reduce waste, and improve quality.

3. Artificial Intelligence: Information technology enables the development of advanced artificial intelligence systems that can learn from data and make decisions. AI can be used to optimize production, predict maintenance needs, and improve quality.

4. Robotics: Information technology enables the development of advanced robotics systems that can perform complex tasks with precision and speed. Robotics can be used to automate production processes, reducing the need for human labor and improving efficiency.

5. Cybersecurity: Information technology enables the development of advanced cybersecurity systems that can protect against cyber threats.

IT vs ICT

The terms IT and ICT are often used interchangeably, but there is a subtle difference between the two.

IT (Information Technology) refers to the use of computers, software, and networks to process, store, and transmit data and information. IT is a broad field that includes hardware, software, telecommunications, and databases. IT professionals are responsible for designing, developing, and maintaining computer systems and networks to meet the needs of individuals and organizations.

ICT (Information and Communications Technology) refers to the integration of information technology and telecommunications to enable efficient communication and information sharing. ICT includes all forms of digital communication, such as email, instant messaging, video conferencing, and social media. ICT also includes the use of mobile devices, such as smartphones and tablets, to access information and communicate on-the-go.

ICT (Information and Communications Technology) is a part of IT (Information Technology). IT is a broad field that encompasses various technologies and applications, including hardware, software, telecommunications, and databases. ICT, on the other hand, is a subset of IT that focuses specifically on the integration of information technology and telecommunications to enable efficient communication and information sharing.

ICT includes all forms of digital communication, such as email, instant messaging, video conferencing, and social media. It also includes the use of mobile devices, such as smartphones and tablets, to access information and communicate on-the-go.

ICT is an essential component of IT because it enables the efficient and effective use of technology to communicate and share information. Without ICT, the full potential of IT would not be realized, as communication and collaboration are critical components of most IT systems and applications.

In summary, ICT is a subset of IT that focuses on the integration of information technology and telecommunications to enable efficient communication and information sharing. While IT encompasses a broader range of technologies and applications, ICT is an essential component of IT, enabling the full potential of IT to be realized. IT is focused on the technology used to process, store, and transmit data and information, while ICT is focused on the use of technology to enable communication and information sharing.

IT in our Daily life

Information technology (IT) has had a profound impact on our daily lives, transforming the way we live, work, and communicate. Here are some ways in which IT affects our daily lives:

1. Communication: IT has revolutionized the way we communicate, making it faster, easier, and more convenient. We can now communicate with people all over the world in real-time using email, instant messaging, video conferencing, and social media. Communication would be much slower and less convenient without IT. We would have to rely on traditional methods of communication,

such as postal mail and telephones, which would be much slower and less efficient.

2. Work: IT has transformed the way we work, making it more efficient and productive. We can now work remotely, access data and applications from anywhere, and collaborate with colleagues in real-time. Work would be much less efficient without IT. We would have to rely on manual processes and paper-based systems, which would be much slower and more prone to errors.

3. Education: IT has transformed education by making it more accessible and interactive. Online courses, e-books, and educational software have made learning more flexible and convenient. Education would be less accessible without IT. We would have to rely on physical books and in-person classes, which would be less flexible and accessible to people in remote areas.

4. Entertainment: Entertainment would be less varied and accessible without IT. We would have to rely on physical media, such as DVDs and CDs, and traditional forms of entertainment, such as live performances and books. IT has transformed the entertainment industry, providing people with access to a wide range of content, including movies, music, and games. We can now stream movies and TV shows, listen to music online, and play games with people from all over the world.

5. Shopping: Shopping would be less convenient without IT. We would have to physically visit stores to purchase products, which would be more time-consuming and less efficient. IT has transformed the way we shop, making it easier and more convenient to buy products and services online. We can now shop from anywhere, at any time, and have products delivered directly to our doorstep.

6. Healthcare: IT has improved healthcare by making it easier to access medical records, share information between healthcare providers, and monitor patients remotely. Healthcare would be less efficient without IT. Medical records would be stored on paper, making it more difficult to access and share information between healthcare providers.

Life without IT would be much slower, less efficient, and less convenient. IT has become an integral part of our daily lives, transforming the way we live, work, and communicate. As technology continues to advance, we can expect to see even more significant changes in our daily lives.

Discussion Guide

1. How do you think will you be able to live for a few days as a student, professional or entrepreneur without a mobile phone or internet connection?
2. Through face-to-face or online surveys, ask 5 friends what they think of IT and what an IT specialist does. Discuss with others learners what are the misconceptions on IT.
3. Explain how IT's evolution has impacted the evolution of humankind.
4. Write down five (5) obsolete IT technologies in your school or workplace .

Activity Guide

1. Using a spider web matrix, illustrate the types of IT and their connectivity in your workplace or school.
2. Using the internet, create a timeline of the evolution of IT leading to what it is today.
3. Using old and new actual technology or IT tool equipment, demonstrate or explain how the innovation or advancement provides better results of its function or impacts (for example, comparing an old to a new pc).

Chapter 2: What is a Computer?

How does a Computer Work?

A computer is an electronic device that processes, stores, and retrieves data. It can perform various tasks, including calculations, data processing, word processing, and multimedia presentations. Computers consist of two primary components: hardware and software. The hardware includes physical components such as the central processing unit (CPU), memory, storage devices, input/output devices, and other peripherals. The software includes the programs and applications that run on the computer, such as the operating system, productivity software, and games. Computers can be used for a wide range of purposes, including personal, educational, commercial, and scientific applications.

The Input-Process-Output (IPO) model is a framework used to describe the flow of information through a system. It is commonly used in computer science, engineering, and other fields to analyze and design systems.

In the IPO model, inputs are the data or information that is entered into a system. This can include data entered by a user, data from sensors, or data from other sources.

The process is the set of operations or actions that are performed on the input data to produce the desired output. This can include calculations, data manipulation, or other operations.

The output is the result or outcome of the process. This can be in the form of data, information, or a physical product.

The IPO model can be used to analyze and design systems by identifying the inputs, processes, and outputs and determining how they interact with each other. This can help to identify areas for improvement or optimization in the system.

Macintosh Apple, US, 1984

A computer workflow refers to the sequence of steps or tasks that are performed by a computer system to complete a specific process or project. It involves the use of software applications, data, and hardware components to automate and streamline the flow of work.

HOW COMPUTER WORKS

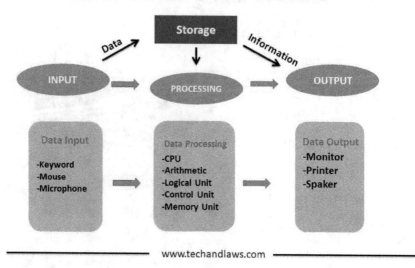

www.techandlaws.com

A computer workflow typically involves the following components:

1. Input: Data or information is entered into the computer system through various input devices such as a keyboard, mouse, or scanner. Computer data input refers to the process of entering data or information into a computer system using various input devices. This data can include text, numbers, images, audio, and video. The input devices used to enter this data can include keyboards, mice, touchscreens, scanners, microphones, and other devices.

Data input is a critical component of any computer system, as it provides the raw data that is processed and analyzed to produce useful information. The accuracy and completeness of the data input can significantly impact the quality of the output produced by the computer system. Therefore, it is essential to ensure that the data is entered correctly and completely to obtain accurate results.

Various software applications are designed to facilitate data input, such as word processors, spreadsheets, and databases. These applications provide an interface that allows users to input data easily and efficiently. Additionally, some applications include features such as auto-complete, spell-check, and data validation to help ensure the accuracy and completeness of data.

2. Processing: The computer processes the data using software applications and algorithms to perform specific tasks or operations. Computer data processing refers to the manipulation and transformation of raw data into useful information by a computer system. It involves a series of operations and calculations that are performed on the data to produce meaningful output. Data processing can be performed in real-time or batch mode. Real-time processing involves processing data as it is received, while batch processing involves processing data in batches at a later time.

3. Output: The processed data is then presented to the user in a usable format, such as a report, graph, or document. Computer

output refers to the information that is produced by a computer system after processing input data. The output can take various forms, including text, graphics, audio, video, and other multimedia formats.

The output can be presented on various output devices, such as monitors, printers, speakers, and projectors. The output can be in the form of reports, graphs, charts, presentations, or other formats that are suitable for the intended audience.

4. Storage: The data is stored in the computer system for future use or reference. Data is stored in a computer using various types of storage devices. The most common storage devices used in computers are hard disk drives (HDDs), solid-state drives (SSDs), and flash memory.

HDDs use magnetic disks to store data. The disks are coated with a magnetic material that can be magnetized to represent data. The read/write head of the HDD accesses the magnetic disks to read or write data. SSDs use NAND flash memory to store data. Unlike HDDs, SSDs have no moving parts and use a controller to access the data stored in the flash memory. SSDs are faster and more durable than HDDs, but they are also more expensive. Flash memory is used in various storage devices, such as USB flash drives, memory cards, and solid-state drives.

5. Communication: The computer system may communicate with other systems or devices to exchange data or information. computer communication is the process of exchanging information between two or more computers or devices. The communication process involves the following steps:

- Sender: The sender is the device that initiates the communication process. It sends the data or information to the receiver.

- Encoding: The data or information is encoded or converted into a format that can be transmitted over the communication channel.

- Transmission: The encoded data is transmitted over the communication channel, which can be wired or wireless.

- Reception: The receiver device receives the transmitted data.

- Decoding: The received data is decoded or converted back to its original format

Computer workflows can be designed and optimized to improve productivity, efficiency, and accuracy. They can be used in various industries and applications, such as manufacturing, healthcare, finance, and education.

Classifications

Computers can be classified into several categories based on their size, purpose, and functionality. Here are some common classifications of computers:

1. Supercomputers: These are the fastest and most powerful computers available. They are used for complex scientific and engineering calculations, weather forecasting, and other applications that require massive processing power.

2. Mainframe computers: These are large computers used by organizations for data processing, transaction processing, and other business applications. They can handle multiple users and large amounts of data simultaneously.

3. Minicomputers: These are smaller than mainframe computers but larger than microcomputers. They were popular in the 1970s and 1980s and were used for scientific and engineering applications.

4. Microcomputers: These are personal computers or desktop computers that are commonly used in homes, offices, and schools. They are small, affordable, and easy to use.

5. Workstations: These are high-performance computers used for specialized applications such as video editing, graphic design, and scientific simulations.

6. Embedded computers: These are computers that are built into other devices such as cars, appliances, and medical equipment. They are designed to perform specific functions and are often used in industrial and commercial applications.

7. Mobile computers: These are portable computers such as laptops, tablets, and smartphones that are designed for mobility and convenience.

These are some common classifications of computers, but there are many other types of computers as well, such as servers, gaming computers, and virtual reality systems.

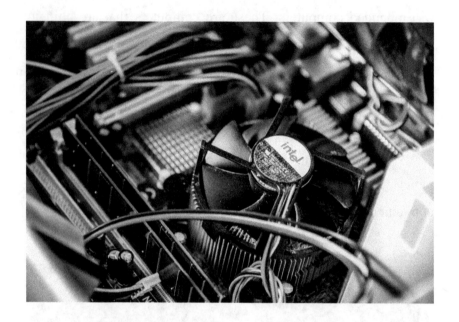

Computers can be classified according to their interface or the way users interact with them. Here are some common classifications of computers based on interface:

1. Desktop computers: These are computers designed to be used on a desk or table and usually consist of a separate monitor, keyboard, and mouse.

2. Laptop computers: These are portable computers that are designed to be used on the go. They have a built-in screen, keyboard, and touchpad or trackpad.

3. Tablet computers: These are portable devices that are designed to be used with a touchscreen interface. They are smaller and more lightweight than laptops and are often used for browsing the internet, reading eBooks, and watching videos.

4. All-in-one computers: These are computers that combine the monitor and computer components into a single unit. They have a smaller footprint than desktop computers and are often used in homes and offices.

Evolution of Computers

There are hundreds of people who have made significant contributions to the field of computing. The following sections describe the main founders of computing, computers, and the computers we use today.

Charles Babbage was considered the father of computing after his conception and invention of the Analytic Engine in 1837. The analytical engine included an ALU (arithmetic logic unit), a basic flow controller, and integrated memory, which was called the first general purpose computer concept. Unfortunately, this computer was not built during Charles Babbage's lifetime due to financial problems. However, in 1910, the youngest son of Charles Babbage, Henry Babbage, completed part of a machine that could perform basic calculations. In 1991, the Science Museum in London built a working version of Analytical Engine No. 2. That version incorporated Babbage's improvements that he developed when creating the Analytical Engine. Although Babbage did not complete his invention in his lifetime, his radical ideas and computer concepts make him the father of computer science.

Several people can be considered the father of the computer, including Alan Turing, John Atanasoff, and John von Neumann. However, we consider Konrad Zu the father of the computer Z1, Z2, Z3 and Z4. Between 1936 and 1938, Konrad Zuse created the

Z1 in his parents' living room. The Z1 had over 30,000 metal parts and was the first electro mechanical binary programmable computer. In 1939, Zuse was commissioned by the German Army with the Z2, which was largely based on the Z1. He later completed Z3 in May 1941; The Z3 was a revolutionary computer for its time and is considered the first electromechanical and programmable computer. Finally, on July 12, 1950, Zuse completed and shipped the Z4 computer, the first commercial computer.

Henry Edward Roberts coined the term "personal computer" and is considered the father of the modern personal computer after he released the Altair 8800 on December 19, 1974. It was later featured on the cover of Popular Electronics in 1975, making it a sudden success. The computer was available as a package for $439 or assembled for $621 and included several add-ons such as a memory card and interface cards. By August 1975, more than 5,000 Altair 8800 personal computers had been sold, starting the personal computer revolution.

The evolution of computer technology is often divided into five generations.

Five Generations of Computers

Generations of computers	Generations timeline	Evolving hardware
First generation	1940s-1950s	Vacuum tube based
Second generation	1950s-1960s	Transistor based
Third generation	1960s-1970s	Integrated circuit based
Fourth generation	1970s-present	Microprocessor based
Fifth generation	The present and the future	Artificial intelligence based

First Generation of Computers

The main characteristics of first generation of computers (1940s-1950s)

- Main electronic component – vacuum tube
- Main memory – magnetic drums and magnetic tapes
- Programming language – machine language
- Power – consumes a lot of electricity and generates a lot of heat.
- Speed and size – very slow and very large in size (often taking up the entire room).
- Input/output devices – punched cards and paper tapes
- Examples – ENIAC, UNIVAC1, IBM 650, IBM 701, etc.
- Quantity – there were about 100 different vacuum tube computers produced between 1942 and 1963.

Second Generation of Computers

The main characteristics of second generation of computers (1950s-1960s)

- Main electronic component – transistor
- Memory – magnetic core and magnetic tape / disk
- Programming language – assembly language
- Power and size – low power consumption, generated less heat, and smaller in size (in comparison with the first generation computers).
- Speed – improvement of speed and reliability (in comparison with the first generation computers).
- Input/output devices – punched cards and magnetic tape.
- Examples – IBM 1401, IBM 7090 and 7094, UNIVAC 1107, etc.

Third Generation of Computers

The main characteristics of third generation of computers (1960s-1970s)

- Main electronic component – integrated circuits (ICs)
- Memory – large magnetic core, magnetic tape / disk

- Programming language – high level language (FORTRAN, BASIC, Pascal, COBOL, C, etc.)
- Size – smaller, cheaper, and more efficient than second generation computers (they were called minicomputers).
- Speed – improvement of speed and reliability (in comparison with the second generation computers).
- Input / output devices – magnetic tape, keyboard, monitor, printer, etc.
- Examples – IBM 360, IBM 370, PDP-11, UNIVAC 1108, etc.

Fourth Generation of Computers

The main characteristics of fourth generation of computers (1970s-present)

- Main electronic component – very large-scale integration (VLSI) and microprocessors
- VLSI– thousands of transistors on a single microchip.
- Memory – semiconductor memory (such as RAM, ROM, etc.
- RAM (random-access memory) – a type of data storage (memory element) used in computers that temporarily stores programs and data (volatile: its contents are lost when the computer is turned off).

- ROM (read-only memory) – a type of data storage used in computers that permanently stores data and programs (non-volatile: its contents are retained even when the computer is turned off).
- Programming language – high level language (Python, C#, Java, JavaScript, Rust, Kotlin, etc.).A mix of both third- and fourth-generation languages
- Size – smaller, cheaper and more efficient than third generation computers.
- Speed – improvement of speed, accuracy, and reliability (in comparison with the third generation computers)
- Input / output devices – keyboard, pointing devices, optical scanning, monitor, printer, etc.
- Network – a group of two or more computer systems linked together.
- Examples – IBM PC, STAR 1000, APPLE II, Apple Macintosh, etc.

Fifth Generation of Computers

The main characteristics of fifth generation of computers (the present and the future)

- Main electronic component: based on artificial intelligence, uses the Ultra Large-Scale Integration (ULSI) technology and parallel processing method.
- ULSI – millions of transistors on a single microchips
- Parallel processing method – use two or more microprocessors to run tasks simultaneously.
- Language – understand natural language (human language).

- Power – consume less power and generate less heat
- Speed – remarkable improvement of speed, accuracy and reliability (in comparison with the fourth generation computers)
- Size – portable and small in size, and have a huge storage capacity.
- Input / output device – keyboard, monitor, mouse, trackpad (or touchpad), touchscreen, pen, speech input (recognise voice / speech), light scanner, printer, etc.
- Example – modern desktops, laptops, tablets, smartphones, etc.

Major Timeline in the History of Computers

Here is a timeline of the major events in the history of computers:

1801: Joseph Marie Jacquard invents a mechanical loom that uses punched cards to control the weaving process.

1822: Charles Babbage designs a mechanical computer called the Difference Engine, which is intended to calculate polynomial functions.

1837: Charles Babbage designs an improved version of the Difference Engine called the Analytical Engine, which is capable of performing any calculation that can be defined by a set of instructions.

1843: Ada Lovelace, a mathematician and writer, publishes a paper describing the potential use of the Analytical Engine for more than just mathematical calculations, suggesting that it could be used to compose music and create graphics.

1890: Herman Hollerith develops an electromechanical tabulating machine that uses punched cards to process data, which is used in the 1890 US Census.

1937: John Atanasoff and Clifford Berry develop the Atanasoff-Berry Computer, which uses binary digits to represent data and performs calculations using electronic switches.

1939: John V. Atanasoff and Clifford Berry develop the first electronic computer prototype, called the Atanasoff-Berry Computer (ABC).

1941: Konrad Zuse develops the world's first programmable computer, the Z3.

1943: Colossus, the world's first electronic digital programmable computer, is developed by Tommy Flowers and his team at Bletchley Park in the UK to break German codes during World War II.

1945: John von Neumann develops the concept of a stored-program computer, which allows instructions and data to be stored in the same memory.

1946: ENIAC (Electronic Numerical Integrator and Computer), the first general-purpose electronic computer, was developed by John Mauchly and J. Presper Eckert at the University of Pennsylvania.

1947: The first transistor, a key component of modern electronics, was invented by William Shockley, John Bardeen, and Walter Brattain at Bell Labs.

1951: The first commercially available computer, the UNIVAC I, is delivered to the United States Census Bureau.

1952: Grace Hopper develops the first compiler, a program that translates high-level programming languages into machine code.

1953: IBM introduces the IBM 701, the first large-scale electronic computer designed for scientific calculations.

1958: Jack Kilby at Texas Instruments invents the integrated circuit, which allows multiple transistors to be placed on a single chip.

1960: The first computer operating system, the Compatible Time-Sharing System (CTSS), is developed at MIT.

1964: IBM introduces the System/360, a family of compatible computers that allows users to upgrade to more powerful models without changing software.

1969: ARPANET, the precursor to the internet, is developed by the US Department of Defense's Advanced Research Projects Agency (ARPA).

1971: Intel introduces the first microprocessor, the Intel 4004, which contains all the components of a central processing unit (CPU) on a single chip.

1975: The Altair 8800, the first commercially successful personal computer, is introduced by MITS.

1981: IBM introduces the IBM PC, which becomes the standard for personal computers.

1984: Apple introduces the Macintosh, the first commercially successful computer with a graphical user interface (GUI).

1991: Linus Torvalds releases the first version of the Linux operating system, which is based on the Unix operating system.

1993: The first web browser, Mosaic, is released by the National Center for Supercomputing Applications (NCSA) at the University of Illinois.

1995: Microsoft releases Windows 95, which includes a new user interface and support for long filenames.

1998: Google is founded by Larry Page and Sergey Brin, offering a new approach to search engine technology.

2001: Apple introduces the iPod, a portable digital music player that revolutionizes the music industry.

2003: The first version of WordPress, a popular content management system (CMS), is released.

2004: Facebook was founded by Mark Zuckerberg, initially as a social network for college students.

2007: Apple introduces the iPhone, a revolutionary smartphone that combines a mobile phone, music player, and internet device in one.

2008: Google releases the first version of the Android operating system, which becomes the most popular mobile operating system in the world.

2010: Apple introduces the iPad, a tablet computer that becomes the most popular tablet in the world.

2011: IBM's Watson computer defeats human contestants on Jeopardy!, demonstrating the power of artificial intelligence.

2015: Microsoft releases Windows 10, which includes a new user interface and support for multiple devices.

2016: Google's AlphaGo computer defeats the world champion in the game of Go, demonstrating the power of deep learning and artificial intelligence.

2017: Intel releases the first consumer-grade processors with more than four cores, offering increased processing power for demanding applications.

2018: GDPR (General Data Protection Regulation) comes into effect in the European Union, regulating the collection, use, and storage of personal data by companies.

2019: Quantum computers become more widely available, with companies like IBM, Google, and Microsoft offering cloud-based quantum computing services.

2020: The COVID-19 pandemic leads to a surge in remote work and online learning, highlighting the importance of technology for communication and collaboration.

2021: Apple releases the M1 chip, which is designed specifically for Mac computers and offers increased performance and energy efficiency.

2022: The first consumer-grade foldable smartphones become available, offering a new form factor for mobile devices.

2023: The first autonomous vehicles become available to consumers, offering a new level of convenience and safety for transportation.

By 2024 onwards, virtual reality and augmented reality technologies will become more widely used in industries such as gaming, education, and healthcare. Likewise, autonomous commercial drones may become available, offering new possibilities for delivery and transportation. Further ahead of time, artificial intelligence will become more advanced, with machine learning algorithms becoming more sophisticated and capable of performing complex tasks. In another decade, it is expected that quantum computing will become more mainstream, with companies developing new applications.

Computer Hardwares

Computer hardware refers to the physical components of a computer system that can be seen and touched. Computer hardware is essential for a computer system to function properly. The components work together to perform various tasks and enable the user to interact with the computer.

Hardware Categories

There are several categories of computer hardware, including:

1. Input devices: These include devices that allow the user to input commands and data into the computer, such as a keyboard, mouse, scanner, and microphone.

2. Output devices: These include devices that allow the computer to display output and produce sound, such as a monitor, printer, and speakers.

3. Storage devices: These include devices that store data and information, such as a hard disk drive (HDD), solid-state drive (SSD), USB flash drive, and memory card.

4. Processing devices: These include devices that perform calculations and processing tasks, such as the central processing unit (CPU) and graphics processing unit (GPU).

5. Communication devices: These include devices that allow the computer to communicate with other devices and networks, such as a network interface card (NIC), modem, and router.

6. Cooling devices: These include devices that help keep the computer's components cool, such as fans, heatsinks, and liquid cooling systems.

7. Power devices: These include devices that provide power to the computer's components, such as a power supply unit (PSU) and uninterruptible power supply (UPS).

Parts of a Desktop Computer

The main parts of a desktop computer are:

1. Central Processing Unit (CPU): This is the "brain" of the computer that performs most of the processing and calculations.

2. Random Access Memory (RAM): This is the temporary memory that the computer uses to store data that is currently being used.

3. Hard Disk Drive (HDD) or Solid State Drive (SSD): This is the permanent storage device that stores the computer's operating system, programs, and data.

4. Motherboard: This is the main circuit board that connects all of the computer's components together.

5. Power Supply Unit (PSU): This provides power to the computer's components.

6. Graphics Processing Unit (GPU): This is a specialized processor that is designed to handle graphics-intensive tasks, such as gaming and video editing.

7. Sound card: This is a hardware component that allows the computer to produce sound.

8. Network interface card (NIC): This is a hardware component that allows the computer to connect to a network.

9. Input devices: These include devices such as a keyboard, mouse, and touchscreen that allow the user to input commands and data into the computer.

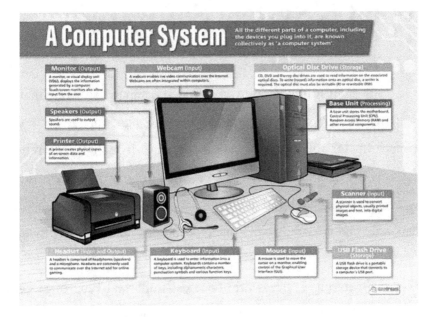

10. Output devices: These include devices such as a monitor, printer, and speakers that allow the computer to display output and produce sound.

11. Optical drives: These include devices such as CD, DVD, and Blu-ray drives that allow the computer to read and write optical discs.

12. Cooling systems: These include fans, heatsinks, and liquid cooling systems that help keep the computer's temperature.

What is System Software?

System software refers to a type of computer software that is designed to manage and control the computer hardware and provide a platform for running application software. It includes operating systems, device drivers, firmware, and utility programs. System software is essential for managing and controlling the computer hardware and providing a platform for running application software.

Operating systems are the most important type of system software. They provide a platform for running application software and manage the computer's resources, such as memory, storage, and processing power. Examples of operating systems include Windows, macOS, Linux, and Android.

Device drivers are another type of system software that allows the operating system to communicate with hardware devices, such as printers, scanners, and video cards. They provide a standardized interface for the operating system to interact with the hardware, allowing the hardware to function properly.

Firmware is a type of system software that is embedded in hardware devices, such as motherboards, hard drives, and routers. It provides low-level control over the hardware and is responsible for initializing the device when it is first powered on.

Utility programs are a type of system software that provides tools for managing and optimizing the computer system. Examples of utility programs include antivirus software, disk cleanup tools, and system optimization tools.

An operating system (OS) is a type of computer software that manages and controls the computer hardware and software resources. The operating system works by managing and controlling the computer hardware and software resources, providing a platform for running application software, and providing a user interface for interacting with the computer.

Some of the key functions of an operating system include:
- Managing computer resources such as memory, CPU, and storage
- Providing a user interface for interacting with the computer
- Managing files and directories
- Providing security and access control
- Managing input and output devices such as keyboards, mice, and printers
- Providing networking capabilities for communication between computers

Examples of popular operating systems include Microsoft Windows, macOS, Linux, and Android. The choice of operating system depends on the specific needs and preferences of the user, as well as the hardware and software requirements of the computer system.

An operating system (OS) works by managing and controlling the computer hardware and software resources. It provides a platform for running application software and acts as an intermediary between the computer hardware and the user.

When the computer is powered on, the operating system is loaded into memory from the hard drive or other storage device. The operating system then initializes the computer hardware, such as the CPU, memory, and storage devices, and provides a user interface for interacting with the computer.

The operating system manages the computer's resources, such as memory, storage, and processing power, by allocating them to different applications and processes as needed. It also manages input and output devices such as keyboards, mice, and printers, and provides networking capabilities for communication between computers.

The operating system provides a file system for managing files and directories, and provides security and access control to ensure that only authorized users have access to the computer system and its resources.

Application software runs on top of the operating system, using the resources provided by the operating system to perform specific tasks. The operating system manages the interaction between the application software and the computer hardware, ensuring that the application software can run smoothly and efficiently.

Device drivers are software programs that allow the operating system to communicate with hardware devices, such as printers, scanners, and video cards. They provide a standardized interface for the operating system to interact with the hardware, allowing the hardware to function properly.

Device drivers act as a bridge between the hardware and the operating system. They translate the commands from the operating system into a language that the hardware can understand. They also provide a layer of abstraction that shields the operating system from the details of the hardware, making it easier to develop software that works with a wide range of hardware devices.

Device drivers are typically developed by the manufacturer of the hardware device and are included with the device or can be downloaded from the manufacturer's website. They are essential for ensuring that hardware devices work properly with the operating system and that the computer system runs smoothly.

Firmware is a type of software that is embedded in hardware devices, such as motherboards, hard drives, and routers. It provides low-level control over the hardware and is responsible for initializing the device when it is first powered on.

Firmware is typically stored in non-volatile memory, such as read-only memory (ROM) or flash memory, which means that it is retained even when the device is powered off. It provides a layer of abstraction between the hardware and the operating system, allowing the operating system to interact with the hardware without needing to know the details of how it works.

Firmware can be updated or upgraded by the manufacturer of the hardware device to fix bugs, add new features, or improve performance. Firmware updates are typically provided as downloads from the manufacturer's website or as part of software updates for the device. It is important to keep firmware up to date to ensure that the hardware device is functioning properly and securely.

Software utilities are a type of software that provides tools for managing and optimizing the computer system. They are designed to perform specific tasks that are not covered by the operating system or other application software. Some common types of software utilities include:

1. Antivirus software: This type of utility program is designed to detect and remove viruses, malware, and other malicious software that can harm the computer system.

2. Disk cleanup tools: These tools help to free up space on the hard drive by removing unnecessary files and temporary files that can accumulate over time.

3. System optimization tools: These tools are designed to improve the performance of the computer system by optimizing the use of system resources, such as memory and CPU.

4. Backup and recovery tools: These tools help to protect important data by creating backups of files and folders, and providing the ability to recover data in case of a system failure or data loss.

5. File compression tools: These tools help to reduce the size of files and folders by compressing them, which can save disk space and make it easier to transfer files over the internet.

6. File recovery tools: These tools help to recover deleted or lost files and folders, which can be useful in case of accidental deletion or system failure.

System Functions

The system function refers to the overall purpose or role of a computer system. It encompasses the various components of the computer system, including the hardware, software, and user interface, and how they work together to achieve the desired outcome.

The system function can vary depending on the specific type of computer system and its intended use. For example, the system function of a personal computer may be to provide a platform for running productivity software, browsing the internet, and storing personal files. The system function of a server may be to provide network services, such as file sharing, email, and web hosting, to other computers on the network.

In general, the system function of a computer system is to provide a platform for performing specific tasks or functions, such as data processing, communication, or entertainment. The system function is determined by the needs and requirements of the user or organization using the computer system, and may evolve over time as technology and user needs change.

OS Functions

An operating system is a software program that manages computer hardware and software resources and provides common services for computer programs. It acts as an intermediary between the computer user and the computer hardware, allowing the user to interact with the computer system effectively. It controls various tasks such as memory allocation, process management, file system management, device management, and user interface management. Examples of popular operating systems include Microsoft Windows, macOS, Linux, and Android. The major functions of operating systems include:

1. Resource management: Operating systems manage the computer's resources, such as memory, CPU, and storage, and allocate them to different applications and processes as needed.

2. Process management: Operating systems manage the execution of processes and threads, ensuring that they run smoothly and efficiently and that they do not interfere with each other.

3. Memory management: Operating systems manage the computer's memory, ensuring that it is used efficiently and that there is enough memory available for running applications and processes.

4. File management: Operating systems provide a file system for managing files and directories, including creating, deleting, and modifying files, and providing access control and security for files.

5. Device management: Operating systems manage input and output devices such as keyboards, mice, and printers, and provide device drivers to allow the operating system to communicate with hardware devices.

6. User interface: Operating systems provide a user interface for interacting with the computer, including graphical user interfaces (GUIs), command-line interfaces (CLIs), and touch interfaces.

7. Security: Operating systems provide security features such as access control, authentication, and encryption, to protect the computer system and its resources from unauthorized access and malicious attacks.

In totality, the major functions of operating systems are to manage and control the computer hardware and software resources, provide a platform for running application software, and provide a user interface for interacting with the computer.

Resource Management

Operating systems (OS) are responsible for managing the computer's resources, such as memory, CPU, and storage, and allocating them to different applications and processes as needed. Resource management is a critical function of the OS, as it ensures that the computer system runs smoothly and efficiently. OS resource management is a critical function of operating systems. It ensures that the computer system runs smoothly and efficiently, and that resources

Memory management is an important aspect of OS resource management. The OS manages the computer's memory, ensuring that it is used efficiently and that there is enough memory available for running applications and processes. The OS allocates memory to different applications and processes, and releases memory when it is no longer needed.

CPU management is another important aspect of OS resource management. The OS manages the CPU, ensuring that it is used efficiently and that there is enough processing power available for running applications and processes. The OS schedules processes and threads to run on the CPU, and ensures that they do not interfere with each other.

Storage management is also an important aspect of OS resource management. The OS manages the computer's storage devices, ensuring that data is stored and retrieved efficiently and that there is enough storage space available for storing files and other data. The OS provides a file system for managing files and directories, including creating, deleting, and modifying files, and providing access control and security for files.

Device management is another important aspect of OS resource management. The OS manages input and output devices such as keyboards, mice, and printers, and provides device drivers to allow the OS to communicate with hardware devices. The OS ensures that devices are used efficiently and that there is enough bandwidth available for communicating with devices.

Process Management

Process management is a critical function of operating systems (OS). It involves managing the execution of processes and threads, ensuring that they run smoothly and efficiently and that they do not interfere with each other.

Processes are programs that are executed by the CPU. Each process has its own memory space and resources, such as files and network connections. The OS manages the execution of processes, ensuring that they have access to the resources they need and that they do not interfere with each other.

Thread management is another important aspect of OS process management. Threads are lightweight processes that share the same memory space and resources as their parent process. The OS manages the execution of threads, ensuring that they run smoothly and efficiently and that they do not interfere with each other.

The OS provides a scheduler to manage the execution of processes and threads. The scheduler determines which process or thread should run on the CPU at any given time, based on priorities and other factors. The scheduler ensures that processes and threads are executed fairly and efficiently, and that they do not interfere with each other.

The OS also provides mechanisms for interprocess communication (IPC), which allows processes and threads to communicate with each other and share data. IPC mechanisms include shared memory, message passing, and pipes.

Process management also includes process creation and termination. The OS provides mechanisms for creating new processes, and for terminating processes.

In short, process management is a critical function of operating systems. It ensures that processes and threads run smoothly and efficiently, and that they do not interfere with each other. It also provides mechanisms for interprocess communication and process creation and termination.

Memory Management

Memory management is a critical function of operating systems (OS). It involves managing the computer's memory, ensuring that it is used efficiently and that there is enough memory available for running applications and processes.

The OS manages memory by allocating and deallocating memory to different applications and processes as needed. It also provides mechanisms for memory protection and virtual memory.

Memory allocation involves assigning blocks of memory to processes and applications. The OS keeps track of which blocks of memory are in use and which are free, and allocates memory to processes and applications as needed. The OS also provides mechanisms for sharing memory between processes and applications.

Memory deallocation involves releasing blocks of memory that are no longer needed by processes and applications. The OS keeps track of which blocks of memory are in use and which are free, and releases memory that is no longer needed. This helps to ensure that memory is used efficiently and that there is enough memory available for other processes and applications.

Memory protection is another important aspect of OS memory management. The OS provides mechanisms for protecting memory from unauthorized access and modification. This helps to ensure the security and integrity of the computer system and its resources.

Virtual memory is another important aspect of OS memory management. Virtual memory allows the computer to use more memory than is physically available by using disk space as a temporary storage area for memory. The OS manages virtual memory by swapping memory pages between physical memory and disk, as needed.

In short, memory management is a critical function of operating systems. It ensures that memory is used efficiently and that there is enough memory available for running applications and processes. It also provides mechanisms for memory protection and virtual memory, which help to ensure the security and integrity of the computer system and its resources.

CPU Management

An operating system (OS) manages the CPU by scheduling processes and threads to run on the CPU, ensuring that they run smoothly and efficiently and that they do not interfere with each other. An OS manages the CPU by providing mechanisms for interprocess communication and interrupt handling, and managing power consumption to conserve energy and extend battery life.

The OS provides a scheduler to manage the execution of processes and threads. The scheduler determines which process or thread should run on the CPU at any given time, based on priorities and other factors. The scheduler ensures that processes and threads are executed fairly and efficiently, and that they do not interfere with each other.

The OS also provides mechanisms for interprocess communication (IPC), which allows processes and threads to communicate with each other and share data. IPC mechanisms include shared memory, message passing, and pipes.

The OS also manages the CPU by providing mechanisms for interrupt handling. Interrupts are signals sent to the CPU by hardware devices, such as keyboards, mice, and network cards, to indicate that they require attention. The OS handles interrupts by suspending the currently running process or thread and executing an interrupt service routine (ISR) to handle the interrupt. Once the ISR is complete, the OS resumes the previously running process or thread.

The OS also manages the CPU by providing mechanisms for power management. Power management involves managing the power consumption of the CPU and other computer components to conserve energy and extend battery life. The OS provides mechanisms for suspending and resuming processes and threads, and for adjusting the CPU clock speed and voltage to reduce power consumption.

Storage Management

Storage management is a critical function of operating systems (OS). It involves managing the computer's storage devices, ensuring that data is stored and retrieved efficiently and that there is enough storage space available for storing files and other data.

The OS manages storage devices by providing a file system for managing files and directories. The file system organizes data into files and directories, and provides mechanisms for creating, deleting, and modifying files. The file system also provides access control and security for files, ensuring that only authorized users have access to them.

The OS also manages storage devices by providing mechanisms for disk management. Disk management involves managing the physical disks and partitions that make up the storage devices. The OS provides tools for formatting disks, creating partitions, and managing disk space.

The OS also provides mechanisms for data backup and recovery. Backup and recovery involves creating copies of important data to protect against data loss due to hardware failure, user error, or other causes. The OS provides tools for creating backups of files and directories, and for recovering data in case of a system failure or data loss.

The OS also manages storage devices by providing mechanisms for disk caching. Disk caching involves temporarily storing frequently accessed data in memory to improve performance. The OS provides mechanisms for caching data to reduce disk access time and improve overall system performance.

It is important to regularly clean up storage devices to free up space and improve performance. However, it is also important to be careful when deleting files and directories, as some files may be necessary for the proper functioning of the OS and applications. Operating systems (OS) provide tools for cleaning up storage devices, such as hard drives, to free up space and improve performance. Here are some common storage cleanup tools provided by OS:

1. Disk Cleanup: This tool is available in Windows OS and helps to free up space on the hard drive by removing temporary files, system files, and other unnecessary files that may accumulate over time.

2. Disk Utility: This tool is available in macOS and allows users to repair disk permissions, verify and repair disk errors, and erase free space on the hard drive.

3. Terminal commands: In Linux and Unix-based OS, users can use terminal commands to clean up storage devices. For example, the "du" command can be used to find out which files and directories are taking up the most space, and the "rm" command can be used to delete files and directories.

4. Third-party cleanup tools: There are also many third-party storage cleanup tools available for different OS, such as CCleaner for Windows and CleanMyMac for macOS.

Operating systems (OS) provide file management tools to manage files and directories on storage devices. File management is a critical function of operating systems. It allows users to organize and manage their files and directories, and provides mechanisms for access control, security, and searching.

The OS provides a file system that organizes files and directories into a hierarchical structure. Files and directories are organized into folders, which can contain subfolders and files. The file system provides a standardized interface for accessing and managing files and directories.

The OS also provides tools for creating, deleting, copying, moving, and renaming files and directories. These tools allow users to organize their files and directories in a way that makes sense for their needs.

The OS also provides mechanisms for file access control and security. Access control allows users to control who can access their files and directories, and what level of access they have. Security mechanisms, such as encryption and password protection, help to protect files and directories from unauthorized access and data theft.

The OS also provides tools for searching for files and directories. These tools allow users to search for files and directories based on their name, file type, size, and other attributes.

There are several different file systems used by various operating systems (OS). Here are some of the most common file systems:

1. FAT (File Allocation Table): FAT is a file system used by older versions of Windows, such as Windows 95, 98, and ME. It is also used by some removable storage devices, such as USB drives.

2. NTFS (New Technology File System): NTFS is a file system used by modern versions of Windows, such as Windows 10, 8, and 7. It provides improved performance, security, and support for larger file sizes and volumes than FAT.

3. HFS+ (Hierarchical File System Plus): HFS+ is a file system used by macOS. It provides support for larger file sizes and volumes than the older HFS file system, and includes features such as journaling and support for case-sensitive file names.

4. APFS (Apple File System): APFS is a file system introduced by Apple in macOS High Sierra. It provides improved performance, security, and support for larger file sizes and volumes than HFS+.

5. ext4 (Fourth Extended File System): ext4 is a file system used by Linux. It provides support for larger file sizes and volumes than the older ext3 file system, and includes features such as journaling and support for extended attributes.

6. exFAT (Extended File Allocation Table): exFAT is a file system designed by Microsoft for use on flash drives and other external

storage devices. It supports large file sizes and is compatible with both Windows and macOS.

7. UDF (Universal Disk Format): UDF (Universal Disk Format) is a file system used for optical media such as DVDs and Blu-ray discs. It was developed to provide a standard file system for optical media that is compatible with different operating systems.

UDF was created by the Optical Storage Technology Association (OSTA) and is supported by most modern operating systems, including Windows, macOS, and Linux. It is designed to support large file sizes and is capable of handling a wide range of file types, including audio and video files.

UDF has several versions, with the latest being UDF 2.60. Each version adds new features and improvements, such as improved error correction and support for larger capacities.

One of the main advantages of UDF is its compatibility with different operating systems. This means that a disc formatted with UDF can be read by different computers and devices, regardless of the operating system they are running. UDF is also designed to provide better error correction and recovery capabilities than other file systems used for optical media.

Device Management

Device management is a critical function of operating systems (OS). It involves managing input and output devices function properly and that there is efficient communication between the OS and the hardware. It also provides mechanisms for device detection and configuration, power management, and device security.

The OS manages devices by providing device drivers, which are software components that allow the OS to communicate with hardware devices. Device drivers provide a standardized interface for the OS to interact with the hardware, allowing the hardware to function properly.

The OS also provides mechanisms for device detection and configuration. When a new device is connected to the computer, the OS detects it and installs the appropriate device driver. The OS also provides tools for configuring and managing devices, such as setting up network connections and configuring printer settings. The OS also manages devices by providing mechanisms for power management. Power management involves managing the power consumption of devices to conserve energy and extend battery life. The OS provides mechanisms for suspending and resuming devices, and for adjusting device power settings to reduce power consumption.

Types of OS

There are several types of operating systems (OS) based on their design, functionality, and usage. Here are some of the most common types:

1. Single-user, single-tasking OS: This type of OS is designed to allow only one user to perform one task at a time. Examples include MS-DOS and early versions of Mac OS.

2. Single-user, multi-tasking OS: This type of OS allows a single user to perform multiple tasks simultaneously. Examples include modern versions of Windows, macOS, and Linux.

3. Multi-user OS: This type of OS allows multiple users to access and use the system simultaneously. Examples include Unix-based OS and server versions of Windows.

4. Real-time OS: This type of OS is designed to process data and respond to events in real-time. Examples include OS used in medical devices, industrial control systems, and aerospace applications.

5. Embedded OS: This type of OS is designed to run on small devices with limited resources, such as smartphones, tablets, and IoT devices.

6. Network OS: This type of OS is designed to manage and control network resources, such as servers, routers, and switches.

7. Mobile OS: This type of OS is designed to run on mobile devices, such as smartphones and tablets. Examples include Android, iOS, and Windows Mobile.

8. Virtualization OS: This type of OS is designed to run virtual machines, allowing multiple OS to run on the same physical machine. Examples include VMware ESXi and Microsoft Hyper-V.

The most popular operating systems (OS) used today are:

1. Windows: Windows is the most widely used OS for desktop and laptop computers, with a market share of over 75%. It is developed by Microsoft and is known for its user-friendly interface, wide range of software compatibility, and strong support for gaming.

2. Android: Android is the most widely used OS for mobile devices, with a market share of over 85%. It is developed by Google and is known for its open-source nature, customizable interface, and wide range of app availability.

3. iOS: iOS is the second most widely used OS for mobile devices, with a market share of over 14%. It is developed by Apple and is known for its user-friendly interface, strong security features, and integration with Apple's ecosystem.

4. macOS: macOS is the second most widely used OS for desktop and laptop computers, with a market share of around 10%. It is developed by Apple and is known for its intuitive interface, strong security features, and seamless integration with other Apple devices.

5. Linux: Linux is an open-source OS that is widely used for servers, supercomputers, and embedded systems. It is known for its stability, security, and flexibility, and is popular among developers and tech enthusiasts.

In simple terms, the popularity of an OS depends on various factors such as user needs, software compatibility, and market trends.

Here is a timeline of some of the major developments in the history of operating systems (OS):

1950s:
- The first electronic computers were developed, but they did not have operating systems.

1960s:

- IBM's OS/360 was released, which was a major step towards standardizing computer systems.
- The first time-sharing systems were developed, which allowed multiple users to access a computer simultaneously.

1970s:

- The UNIX operating system was developed at Bell Labs by Ken Thompson and Dennis Ritchie.
- Microsoft was founded and began developing software for personal computers.

1980s:

- Apple released the Macintosh, which introduced the graphical user interface (GUI) to personal computers.
- IBM released PC-DOS, which was the first operating system for IBM-compatible personal computers.
- Microsoft released MS-DOS, which became the dominant operating system for IBM-compatible personal computers.

1990s:

- Microsoft released Windows 3.0, which was the first version of Windows to gain widespread popularity.

- Linux was released as an open-source operating system.
- Apple released Mac OS X, which was based on UNIX.

2000s:
- Microsoft released Windows XP, which became one of the most popular versions of Windows.
- Apple released macOS, which became popular among creative professionals.
- Linux gained popularity as a server operating system.

2010s:
- Apple released iOS, which became the second most popular mobile operating system.
- Google released Android, which became the most popular mobile operating system.
- Microsoft released Windows 8, which introduced a touch-focused interface.
- Google released Chrome OS, which is a lightweight operating system designed for web-based applications.

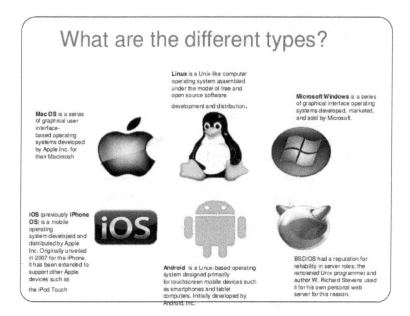

- Microsoft released Windows 10, which introduced a new user interface and new features such as Cortana and the Microsoft Edge browser.

2020s:

- Apple released macOS Big Sur, which introduced a new design and new features such as Control Center and improved Messages app.
- Microsoft released Windows 11, which introduced a new design and new features such as Snap Layouts and Snap Groups.
- Google released Android 12, which introduced a new design and new features such as Material You and improved privacy controls.

Application Systems

Application systems are software programs designed to perform specific tasks or functions for users. These systems are typically developed to meet specific business or organizational needs and are used to automate tasks, improve efficiency, and support decision-making processes.

Application systems can be classified into different types based on their functionality and purpose. Some common types of application systems include:

1. Enterprise Resource Planning (ERP) Systems: These are comprehensive software systems designed to manage all aspects of an organization's operations, including finance, human resources, supply chain, and customer relationship management. ERP (Enterprise Resource Planning) is a type of software system designed to manage and integrate an organization's business processes and data. ERP systems typically include a suite of integrated applications that automate and streamline various business functions such as finance, human resources, supply chain management, customer relationship management, and manufacturing.

The main goal of an ERP system is to provide a centralized view of an organization's data and operations, enabling better decision-making, improved collaboration, and increased efficiency. By integrating various business processes and data into a single system, an ERP system can help organizations reduce costs, eliminate redundancies, and improve productivity.

Some common features of an ERP system include:

- 1. Financial Management: ERP systems typically include modules for managing financial processes such as accounting, budgeting, and financial reporting.

- 2. Human Resources Management: ERP systems can also include modules for managing employee information, payroll, benefits, and performance management.

- 3. Supply Chain Management: ERP systems can help manage the entire supply chain, including procurement, inventory management, and logistics.

- 4. Customer Relationship Management: ERP systems can also include modules for managing customer information, sales, marketing, and customer service.

To simply put it, an ERP system can provide a comprehensive view of an organization's operations, enabling better decision-making and improved efficiency. However, implementing an ERP system can be complex and time-consuming, requiring significant planning, resources,

Some of the key features of an ERP system include:

- Centralized database: An ERP system stores all data in a single, centralized database, eliminating the need for multiple data sources and reducing data redundancy.

- Real-time data: An ERP system provides real-time data on various business functions, allowing managers to make informed decisions based on up-to-date information.

- Automation: An ERP system automates many routine tasks, such as data entry and report generation, which reduces the risk of errors and improves efficiency.

- Customization: An ERP system can be customized to meet the specific needs of an organization, including adding new modules or modifying existing ones.

- Scalability: An ERP system can be scaled up or down depending on the size and needs of an organization.

2. Supply Chain Management (SCM) Systems: These systems are designed to manage the flow of goods and services from suppliers to customers, including procurement, logistics, and inventory management.

Supply chain management (SCM) systems are software applications designed to manage the flow of goods, services, and information from suppliers to customers. SCM systems provide a centralized platform for managing various supply chain functions

such as procurement, inventory management, logistics, transportation, and demand planning.

SCM systems are designed to help organizations improve efficiency, reduce costs, and enhance customer satisfaction by optimizing their supply chain processes. Some of the key features of SCM systems include:

- Procurement Management: SCM systems provide tools for managing the procurement process, including supplier selection, contract management, and purchase order creation.

- Inventory Management: SCM systems help organizations manage their inventory levels by tracking stock levels, identifying slow-moving items, and optimizing replenishment.

- Logistics Management: SCM systems provide tools for managing transportation, warehousing, and distribution, including route optimization, shipment tracking, and delivery scheduling.

- Demand Planning: SCM systems help organizations forecast demand for their products or services, allowing them to optimize production and inventory levels.

- Collaboration: SCM systems enable collaboration between suppliers, manufacturers, and customers, allowing them to share information and coordinate activities more effectively.

To sum it, SCM systems are designed to help organizations manage their supply chain processes more efficiently, reducing costs and improving customer satisfaction. By providing a centralized platform for managing various supply chain functions, SCM systems can help organizations gain a competitive advantage in their industry.

4. Business Intelligence (BI) Systems: These systems are designed to collect, analyze, and present data in a way that supports decision-making processes.

BI systems typically include tools for data visualization, reporting, and analytics. These tools allow users to explore data, identify trends, and generate reports that can be used to support decision-making at all levels of an organization.

Some of the key features of BI systems include:

- Data Integration: BI systems can integrate data from various sources, allowing users to analyze data from multiple systems in a single dashboard.

- Data Visualization: BI systems provide tools for visualizing data, such as charts, graphs, and maps, making it easier to identify trends and patterns in the data.

- Reporting: BI systems allow users to generate reports based on the data, which can be used to support decision-making.

- Self-Service Analytics: BI systems provide self-service analytics tools, allowing users to explore data and generate insights without the need for IT support.

- Predictive Analytics: BI systems can use predictive analytics to forecast future trends and outcomes based on historical data.

5. Content Management Systems (CMS): These systems are designed to manage digital content, including documents, images, and videos. Thus, CMSs are designed to help users create and manage digital content more efficiently, reducing the time and resources required to create and publish content. By providing a centralized platform for managing content, CMSs can help organizations improve their online presence, engage with their audience, and drive business results.

Content Management Systems (CMS) are software applications designed to help users create, manage, and publish digital content, such as web pages, blog posts, and multimedia content. CMSs provide a user-friendly interface for managing content, allowing users to create, edit, and publish content without the need for technical knowledge.

CMSs typically include features such as:

- Content Creation: CMSs provide tools for creating and editing content, including text editors, image and video editors, and templates for designing web pages.

- Content Management: CMSs provide tools for managing content, including organizing content into categories, tagging content for easy searching, and archiving old content.

- Workflow Management: CMSs provide tools for managing the content creation and publishing process, including assigning roles and permissions to users, setting up approval workflows, and tracking changes to content.

- Publishing: CMSs provide tools for publishing content to various channels, such as websites, social media, and email newsletters.

- Analytics: CMSs provide tools for tracking and analyzing content performance, including page views, engagement metrics, and conversion rates.

System Utilities

System utilities are software applications designed to help users manage and optimize their computer systems. These utilities are typically included with the operating system or can be downloaded as third-party software. By using system utilities, users can improve system performance, increase security, and reduce the risk of system failure.

Some common types of system utilities include:

1. Disk Cleanup and Defragmentation: These utilities help users free up disk space by removing unnecessary files and optimizing the placement of files on the hard drive.

2. System Backup and Restore: These utilities allow users to create backup copies of their system files and settings, which can be used to restore the system in case of a hardware failure or software error.

3. Antivirus and Firewall: These utilities help protect the system from malware, viruses, and other security threats.

4. System Maintenance: These utilities help users maintain the health of their system by monitoring system performance, identifying and fixing errors, and updating drivers and software.

5. Registry Cleaners: These utilities help users optimize the Windows registry by removing outdated or unnecessary entries, which can improve system performance.

6. System Information: These utilities provide detailed information about the system hardware and software, including the system configuration, processor speed, and available memory.

Computer Software Applications

A computer software application is a program or set of programs designed to perform a specific task or set of tasks on a

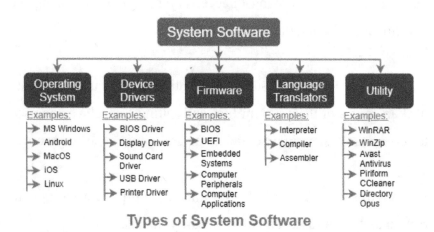

Types of System Software

computer. These applications can be installed on a computer's operating system and can be used to perform a wide range of functions, from word processing to gaming. In simple terms, computer software applications are essential tools for performing various tasks on a computer, and they play a critical role in modern-day computing.

Software applications can be classified into different types based on their functionality and purpose. Some common types of software applications include:

Productivity Softwares

This type of software includes applications such as word processors, spreadsheets, and presentation software, which are used for creating and managing documents, spreadsheets, and presentations.Productivity software is designed to help users work more efficiently and effectively, by providing tools and applications that streamline tasks and improve workflow This type of software includes a variety of tools and applications that are used for creating and managing documents, spreadsheets, presentations, and other types of content.

Some common types of productivity software include:

1. Word processors: These software applications are used for creating and editing text documents, such as letters, reports, and

memos. Examples of popular word processors include Microsoft Word, Google Docs, and Apple Pages.

2. Spreadsheets: These software applications are used for creating and managing numerical data, such as budgets, financial statements, and project plans. Examples of popular spreadsheet software include Microsoft Excel, Google Sheets, and Apple Numbers.

3. Presentation software: These software applications are used for creating and delivering presentations, such as slideshows and multimedia presentations. Examples of popular presentation software include Microsoft PowerPoint, Google Slides, and Apple Keynote.

4. Project management software: These software applications are used for managing projects, tasks, and resources. Examples of popular project management software include Trello, Asana, and Microsoft Project.

5. Note-taking software: These software applications are used for taking and organizing notes, such as meeting notes, to-do lists, and research notes. Examples of popular note-taking software include Evernote, OneNote, and Google Keep.

Communication Software

This type of software includes applications such as email clients, instant messaging software, and video conferencing software, which are used for communicating with others.

Communication software is a type of application software designed to facilitate communication between individuals or groups. This type of software includes a variety of tools and applications that are used for messaging, voice and video calling, email, and other forms of communication to improve collaboration and productivity in both personal and professional settings.

Some common types of communication software include:

1. Email clients: These software applications are used for sending and receiving email messages. Examples of popular email clients include Microsoft Outlook, Gmail, and Apple Mail.

2. Instant messaging software: These software applications are used for real-time messaging between individuals or groups. Examples of popular instant messaging software include WhatsApp, Facebook Messenger, and Slack.

3. Voice and video calling software: These software applications are used for making voice and video calls between individuals or

groups. Examples of popular voice and video calling software include Skype, Zoom, and Google Meet.

4. Web conferencing software: These software applications are used for conducting online meetings and webinars. Examples of popular web conferencing software include GoToMeeting, Cisco Webex, and Microsoft Teams.

5. Social media platforms: These platforms are used for social networking and communication between individuals or groups. Examples of popular social media platforms include Facebook, Twitter, and LinkedIn.

Multimedia Software

This type of software includes applications such as media players, video editing software, and graphic design software, which are used for creating and editing multimedia content.

Multimedia software is a type of application software designed to create, edit, and manage multimedia content, such as images, audio, and video. This type of software includes a variety of tools and applications that are used for creating and editing multimedia content, as well as for playing and managing multimedia files.

Some common types of multimedia software include:

1. Image editing software: These software applications are used for editing and manipulating digital images, such as photos and graphics. Examples of popular image editing software include Adobe Photoshop, GIMP, and CorelDRAW.

2. Audio editing software: These software applications are used for editing and manipulating digital audio files, such as music tracks and sound effects. Examples of popular audio editing software include Audacity, Adobe Audition, and Pro Tools.

3. Video editing software: These software applications are used for editing and manipulating digital video files, such as movies and TV shows. Examples of popular video editing software include Adobe Premiere Pro, Final Cut Pro, and iMovie.

4. Media players: These software applications are used for playing and managing multimedia files, such as music and video files. Examples of popular media players include Windows Media Player, iTunes, and VLC Media Player.

5. 3D modeling software: These software applications are used for creating and manipulating 3D models and animations. Examples of

popular 3D modeling software include Autodesk Maya, Blender, and Cinema 4D.

Utility Software

This type of software includes applications such as antivirus software, disk cleanup software, and backup software, which are used for maintaining and optimizing the computer system. Utility software is a type of application software designed to help users maintain and optimize their computer systems. This type of software includes a variety of tools and applications that are used for system maintenance, security, and optimization. Utility softwares are more commonly known as system utilities.

Gaming Software

This type of software includes applications such as video games and game development software, which are used for playing games or creating games.

Gaming software is a type of application software designed for playing video games on a computer, console, or mobile device.

This type of software includes a variety of tools and applications that are used for creating, managing, and playing video games.

Some common types of gaming software include:

1. Game engines: These software applications are used for creating and managing video games. Examples of popular game engines include Unity, Unreal Engine, and CryEngine.

2. Game development software: These software applications are used for designing and developing video games. Examples of popular game development software include GameMaker Studio, RPG Maker, and Construct.

3. Gaming platforms: These platforms are used for playing and managing video games. Examples of popular gaming platforms include Steam, PlayStation Network, and Xbox Live.

4. Emulators: These software applications are used for running video games on a computer or mobile device that is not designed to play the game. Examples of popular emulators include PCSX2, Dolphin, and MAME.

5. Mods: These software applications are used for modifying existing video games to add new features or change gameplay.

Examples of popular mods include Minecraft mods, Skyrim mods, and Grand Theft Auto mods.

Software Development

Computer software is developed through different methods and approaches. The choice of software application development method depends on the specific project requirements, team size, and other factors. Each method has its own advantages and disadvantages, and it's important to choose the right method for the project to ensure its success. Some of the software development methods are as follows:

1. Waterfall Model
2. Agile Methodology
3. DevOps
4. Rapid Application Development (RAD)
5. Lean Development
6. Scrum

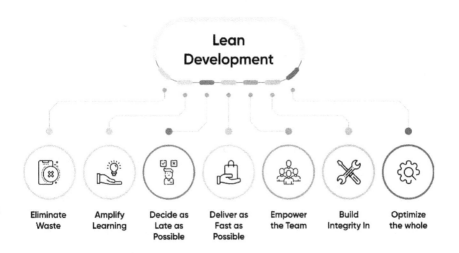

7. Kanban

8. Spiral Model

9. Iterative Model

10. V-Model

11. Extreme Programming (XP)

12. Feature-Driven Development (FDD)

13. Joint Application Development (JAD)

14. Dynamic Systems Development Method (DSDM)

15. Rational Unified Process (RUP)

The most common methods are:

1. Waterfall Model: This is a linear approach to software development that involves a sequence of phases, including requirements gathering, design, implementation, testing, and maintenance. Each phase must be completed before the next one can begin. The waterfall model is best suited for projects with well-defined requirements and a fixed scope.

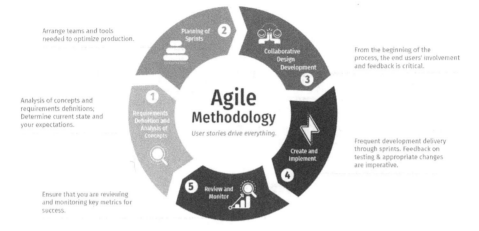

Arrange teams and tools needed to optimize production.

Planning of Sprints 2

Collaborative Design Development

From the beginning of the process, the end users' involvement and feedback is critical.

3

Analysis of concepts and requirements definitions; Determine current state and your expectations.

1 Requirements Definition and Analysis of Concepts

Agile Methodology

User stories drive everything.

Create and Implement

Frequent development delivery through sprints. Feedback on testing & appropriate changes are imperative.

4

5 Review and Monitor

Ensure that you are reviewing and monitoring key metrics for success.

2. Agile Methodology: This is an iterative approach to software development that involves continuous collaboration between the development team and stakeholders. Agile methodology emphasizes flexibility and adaptability, with a focus on delivering working software in short iterations. Scrum and Kanban are two popular frameworks for implementing agile methodology.

3. DevOps: This is a methodology that emphasizes collaboration between development and operations teams to accelerate the software development process. DevOps involves continuous integration, testing, and deployment, with a focus on automation and monitoring.

4. Rapid Application Development (RAD): This is a methodology that emphasizes rapid prototyping and iterative development. RAD

involves developing a working prototype quickly and refining it through multiple iterations based on feedback from stakeholders.

5. Lean Development: This is a methodology that emphasizes minimizing waste and maximizing value. Lean development involves continuous improvement and eliminating unnecessary steps in the software development process.

Cloud Computing and AI

Cloud computing is a technology that allows users to access computing resources, such as servers, storage, and databases, over the internet. Instead of storing data and running applications on a local computer or server, cloud computing allows users to access these resources from a remote location, typically through a web browser or an application programming interface (API).

Cloud computing has become increasingly popular in recent years, as it allows businesses and individuals to access computing resources on demand, without the need for expensive hardware and infrastructure. It also allows for greater flexibility and scalability, as users can quickly and easily scale up or down as their needs change.

Cloud computing is based on a model of shared computing resources, where multiple users can access the same resources simultaneously. This allows for greater efficiency and cost savings, as users only pay for the resources they need, and can quickly scale up or down as their needs change. Cloud computing offers a range of benefits for office environments, including improved collaboration, storage, communication, and backup and recovery.

Cloud Computing

There are three main types of cloud computing:

1. Infrastructure as a Service (IaaS): This provides users with access to virtualized computing resources, such as servers, storage, and networking.

2. Platform as a Service (PaaS): This provides users with a platform for developing, testing, and deploying applications, without the need for infrastructure management.

3. Software as a Service (SaaS): This provides users with access to software applications over the internet, without the need for installation or maintenance.

Cloud computing offers several benefits for office environments, including:

1. Collaboration: Cloud-based productivity suites like Google Workspace (formerly G Suite) and Microsoft Office 365 allow multiple users to collaborate on documents, spreadsheets, and presentations in real-time.

2. Storage: Cloud-based storage solutions like Google Drive, Dropbox, and OneDrive allow users to store and access files from anywhere with an internet connection.

3. Communication: Cloud-based communication tools like Slack and Microsoft Teams allow teams to communicate and collaborate in real-time, regardless of their location.

4. Virtual desktops: Cloud-based virtual desktops like Amazon WorkSpaces and Microsoft Windows Virtual Desktop allow users to access a virtual desktop environment from anywhere with an internet connection.

5. Backup and recovery: Cloud-based backup and recovery solutions like Carbonite and Acronis allow businesses to back up their data to the cloud, protecting against data loss and facilitating disaster recovery.

Artificial Intelligence (AI)

Artificial Intelligence (AI) and computing are closely related, as AI relies heavily on computing power and technology to function. AI is the ability of machines to perform tasks that typically require human intelligence, such as learning, reasoning, and problem-solving. Computing provides the infrastructure and tools needed to develop and deploy AI applications.

AI and computing are used in a wide range of industries, including healthcare, finance, manufacturing, and transportation. Some of the ways AI and computing are used include:

1. Machine learning: This is a type of AI that allows machines to learn from data and improve their performance over time. Machine learning algorithms require significant computing power to process and analyze large datasets.

2. Natural language processing (NLP): This is a type of AI that allows machines to understand and interpret human language. NLP

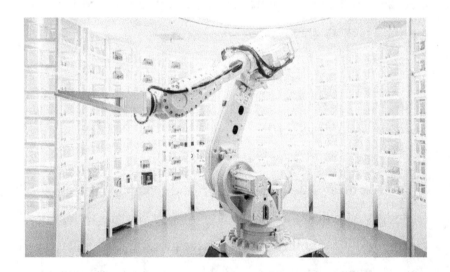

requires significant computing power to process and analyze large amounts of text data.

3. Computer vision: This is a type of AI that allows machines to interpret and understand visual information, such as images and videos. Computer vision requires significant computing power to process and analyze visual data.

4. Robotics: This is a field of AI that involves the development of machines that can perform tasks autonomously. Robotics requires significant computing power to control and operate robots.

5. Cloud computing: This is a technology that allows users to access computing resources over the internet, including AI and machine learning tools. Cloud computing provides the scalability and flexibility needed to support AI applications.

To sum it, AI and computing are closely intertwined, as AI relies on computing power and technology to function. As the field of AI continues to grow and evolve, computing will play an increasingly important role in its development and deployment.

Discussion Guide

1. Enumerate the five (5) types of Software applications according to their usage. Give an example for each type.

2. What are the five most important software development approaches? If you are going to develop a new personal scheduling and time management software, what approach will you use? Why?

3. Do you think Artificial Intelligence will soon replace human beings? Explain.

Activity Guide

1. Create a Google Account. Learn and perform:
   - sending an mail with an attachment
   - using google drive, creating folders, uploading files and sharing files
   - creating a google doc, editing and sharing a doc file
   - creating a google slide presentation, sharing a file and presenting before the class or office using google slide.

2. Using your Facebook Account, learn how to configure security settings, to create a company or product page, and to create a group.

3. Hands-on Workshop. Using a desktop computer set, assemble and disassemble a desktop CPU and learn how to replace the following parts:
   - RAM
   - Processor
   - Hard drive

4. Hands-on Workshop. Using an installer flash drive, effectively install a windows operating system or an OSX into a laptop/ macbook.

5. Hands-on Workshop. Improve your typing skills by using a free online typing program or download Typing Master free software. Perform all typing challenges and achieve at least 32 wpm.

Chapter 3: The Internet

The Internet Defined

The Internet is a global network of computers and other electronic devices that are connected together to exchange information and communicate with each other. It is a decentralized network that allows users to access and share information from anywhere in the world.

The Internet is made up of many different types of networks, including local area networks (LANs), wide area networks (WANs), and the World Wide Web (WWW). The WWW is a collection of interconnected documents and resources that are accessed through the Internet using web browsers. The Internet provides a wide range of services and applications, including email, messaging, file sharing, online gaming, social networking, e-commerce, and online streaming. It has revolutionized the way people communicate, access information, and conduct business. The Internet is maintained and managed by a global community of individuals, organizations, and governments. It operates on a set of protocols and standards, such as the Transmission Control Protocol/Internet Protocol (TCP/IP), that ensure the interoperability and reliability of the network.

How does the Internet Work?

The Internet is a complex network of computers and other electronic devices, and it works by using a set of protocols and standards to facilitate communication and data exchange between these devices. Here is a brief overview of how the Internet works in technical terms:

1. Data transmission: Data is transmitted over the Internet in the form of packets. These packets contain information such as the source and destination addresses, the type of data being transmitted, and error-checking information.

2. Routing: Packets are routed through the network using routers, which are specialized devices that are designed to direct traffic to its destination. Routers use protocols such as the Border Gateway Protocol (BGP) to exchange information about the best routes for data to take.

3. Domain Name System (DNS): The DNS is a hierarchical system that is used to translate human-readable domain names (such as google.com) into IP addresses (such as 172.217.6.174). When a user types a domain name into their web browser, the DNS is used to look up the IP address of the server that hosts the website.

4. Transmission Control Protocol/Internet Protocol (TCP/IP): TCP/IP is a set of protocols that is used to ensure reliable data transmission over the Internet. TCP breaks data into packets and ensures that they are transmitted and received in the correct order, while IP is responsible for routing packets to their destination.

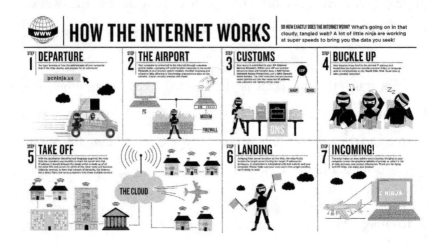

5. Hypertext Transfer Protocol (HTTP): HTTP is a protocol that is used to transfer data over the World Wide Web. When a user requests a web page, their web browser sends an HTTP request to the server that hosts the page. The server responds with an HTTP response, which contains the requested.

What is an IP Address?

An IP address, short for Internet Protocol address, is a unique numerical identifier assigned to every device that is connected to the internet. It is used to identify and communicate with devices on the internet.

An IP address is a 32-bit binary number, but it is usually expressed in human-readable form as a series of four decimal numbers separated by periods. For example, an IP address might be expressed as 192.168.1.1.

There are two types of IP addresses: IPv4 and IPv6. IPv4 addresses are 32 bits long and are expressed in the format described above. However, due to the large number of devices connected to the internet, the available pool of IPv4 addresses is running out.

IPv6 addresses are 128 bits long and are expressed as a series of eight groups of four hexadecimal digits, separated by colons. For example, an IPv6 address might be expressed as *2001:0db8:85a3:0000:0000:8a2e:0370:7334*. IP addresses are used to route data packets between devices on the internet. When a device sends data over the internet, it includes its own IP address and the IP address of the destination device in the packet. Routers use this information to direct the packet to its destination.

What is a Website?

A website is a collection of related web pages that are hosted on a server and can be accessed by users via the internet. A website may contain text, images, videos, and other types of content, and it is typically used to provide information, promote a business or organization, or facilitate communication between individuals or groups.

A website is accessed through a web browser, such as Google Chrome, Safari, or Mozilla Firefox. When a user types a website's domain name or URL (Uniform Resource Locator) into their browser's address bar, the browser sends a request to the server hosting the website. The server responds by sending the requested web page to the user's browser, which displays it on the user's screen.

Websites can vary in complexity and functionality, from simple static websites that provide basic information to complex web applications that allow users to interact with data and perform advanced tasks. Websites can also be designed for different types of devices, such as desktop computers, laptops, tablets, and mobile phones, and they may use different technologies, such as HTML, CSS, JavaScript, and server-side scripting languages like PHP and Python.

A website is a collection of related web pages that are hosted on a server and can be accessed by users via the internet. A domain, on the other hand, is the unique address that is used to identify a website on the internet. In this section, we will explain how websites and domains work together to enable users to access web content.

When a user types a website's domain name or URL (Uniform Resource Locator) into their web browser's address bar, the browser sends a request to a domain name system (DNS) server. The DNS server looks up the IP address associated with the domain name and returns it to the user's browser.

The IP address is a unique identifier that is used to locate the server hosting the website. Once the browser has the IP address, it sends a request to the server, asking for the web page associated with the domain name. The server responds by sending the requested web page back to the user's browser, which displays it on the user's screen.

Domains are registered with domain name registrars, which are organizations authorized to manage and sell domain names. When a user registers a domain name, they are essentially leasing the right to use that domain name for a specified period of time, usually one year. The user can then associate the domain name with a web hosting service, which will host the website's files and make them available to users on the internet.

What is DNS?

DNS stands for Domain Name System. It is a hierarchical system that is used to translate human-readable domain names, such as google.com, into IP (Internet Protocol) addresses, such as 172.217.6.174. DNS is a critical component of the internet infrastructure, allowing users to access websites and other resources using easy-to-remember domain names instead of IP addresses.

When a user types a domain name into their web browser's address bar, the browser sends a request to a DNS server. The DNS server then looks up the IP address associated with the domain name and returns it to the user's browser. The browser then sends a request to the server hosting the website, using the IP address obtained from the DNS server.

DNS operates on a distributed system of servers, with each server responsible for a specific domain or group of domains. The system is hierarchical, with the root DNS servers at the top, followed by top-level domain (TLD) servers, and then authoritative DNS servers for individual domains. When a DNS server receives a request for a domain name that it is not responsible for, it forwards the request to another DNS server higher up in the hierarchy.

DNS servers use a variety of protocols and algorithms to ensure the efficient and reliable resolution of domain names. These include the DNS protocol, which is used for communication between DNS servers, and various caching and load-balancing techniques that help to distribute the workload across multiple servers.

DNS (Domain Name System) is a distributed system that translates domain names into IP addresses. It allows users to access websites and other resources on the internet by using familiar domain names instead of long, complex IP addresses. Here's a simplified explanation of how DNS works:

1. When a user enters a domain name (e.g., www.example.com) into a web browser, the browser sends a request to a DNS resolver (usually provided by the ISP or a third-party DNS service).

2. The resolver checks its local cache to see if it has the corresponding IP address for the domain. If not, it contacts a root DNS server.

3. The root DNS server provides the resolver with the IP address of the Top-Level Domain (TLD) server for the specific domain extension (.com, .net, etc.).

4. The resolver then contacts the TLD server and requests the IP address for the specific domain (www.example.com).

5. The TLD server either responds with the IP address or redirects the resolver to the authoritative DNS server for the domain.

6. The resolver contacts the authoritative DNS server responsible for the domain name in question and requests the IP address.

7. The authoritative DNS server responds with the IP address, and the resolver stores it in its cache for future use.

8. The resolver finally returns the IP address to the user's browser, which can then initiate a connection to the web server associated with that IP address.

Throughout this process, multiple levels of DNS servers are involved, and caching is utilized to accelerate subsequent requests for the same domain. The hierarchical structure of DNS helps distribute the workload and improve efficiency, allowing the internet to handle billions of domain name requests efficiently.

What is a Domain Name?

Domain names are human-readable names that are used to identify websites and other resources on the internet. They are composed of two parts: the top-level domain (TLD) and the second-level domain (SLD).

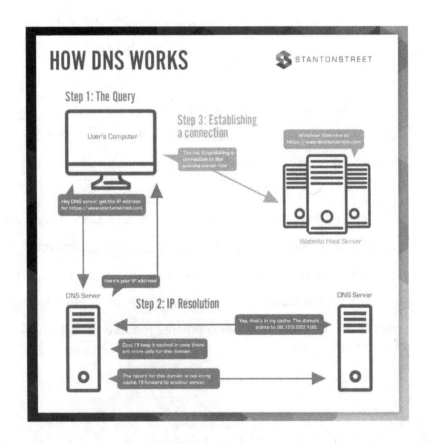

The TLD is the part of the domain name that appears to the right of the dot, such as .com, .org, or .net. There are many different

TLDs available, including country-specific TLDs like .us (United States) and .ca (Canada), as well as generic TLDs like .com, .org, and .net.

The SLD is the part of the domain name that appears to the left of the dot and is chosen by the owner of the domain. For example, in the domain name google.com, "google" is the SLD.

Domain names are used to provide a human-readable address for websites and other resources on the internet. They are easier to remember than IP addresses, which are numerical identifiers used to locate servers on the internet.

Domain names are registered with domain name registrars, which are organizations authorized to manage and sell domain names. When a user registers a domain name, they are essentially leasing the right to use that domain name for a specified period of time, usually one year.

If you want to get your own domain name, you need to follow these steps:

1. Choose a domain registrar: A domain registrar is a company that manages the registration of domain names. There are many domain registrars available, such as GoDaddy, Namecheap, and Google Domains. Choose a registrar that suits your needs and budget.

2. Search for available domain names: Once you have chosen a registrar, use their domain search tool to check if available. If it is not, try different variations or extensions.

3. Choose your domain name: Once you have found an available domain name that you like, select it and add it to your cart.

4. Payment. Pay the domain name.

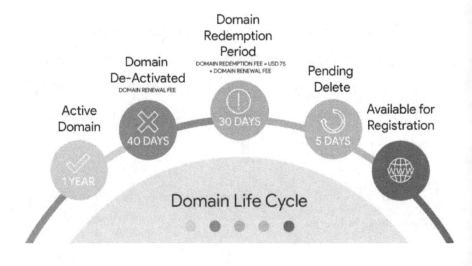

Email

An email, short for electronic mail, is a digital message that is sent and received over the internet. It is a common method of communication used for both personal and professional purposes.

Email messages can contain text, images, attachments, and hyperlinks, and they are typically sent using a specialized email client or webmail service. Email clients are software applications that are installed on a computer or mobile device and are used to manage email messages. Webmail services are web-based applications that allow users to access their email accounts through a web browser.

To send an email, the sender must have a valid email address and access to an email client or webmail service. They compose the message, add any attachments or hyperlinks, and specify the recipient's email address. The email is then sent over the internet to the recipient's email server, which stores the message until the recipient logs in to their email client or webmail service and retrieves it.

Email messages can be sent to a single recipient or to multiple recipients, and they can be organized into folders and searched for later reference. Email is a fast and convenient way to communicate with others, allowing users to send and receive messages from anywhere in the world as long as they have an internet connection.

Email is a complex system that relies on a variety of protocols and standards to ensure the reliable and efficient transmission of messages over the internet. In technical terms, an email is a digital message that is sent and received using a protocol called Simple Mail Transfer Protocol (SMTP). Here is a brief overview of how email works in technical terms:

1. Composing an email: The sender composes the email using an email client or webmail service. The email can contain text, images, attachments, and hyperlinks.

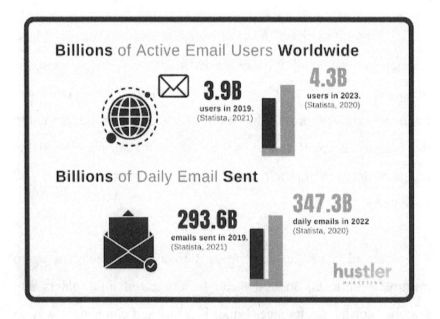

Billions of Active Email Users Worldwide

3.9B users in 2019. (Statista, 2021)

4.3B users in 2023. (Statista, 2020)

Billions of Daily Email Sent

293.6B emails sent in 2019. (Statista, 2021)

347.3B daily emails in 2022 (Statista, 2020)

hustler MARKETING

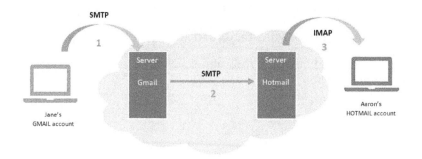

2. Sending the email: When the sender clicks the "send" button, the email client or webmail service uses SMTP to send the email to the recipient's email server. The email is broken down into packets and sent over the internet to the recipient's email server.

3. Receiving the email: When the recipient's email server receives the email, it stores it in a mailbox until the recipient logs in to their email client or webmail service and retrieves it. The email server uses the Internet Message Access Protocol (IMAP) or Post Office Protocol (POP) to allow the recipient to access their mailbox and retrieve their email.

4. Reading the email: When the recipient opens the email, their email client or webmail service uses the Hypertext Markup Language (HTML) or Plain Text format to display the contents of the email on the recipient's screen.

5. Replying to or forwarding the email: The recipient can reply to or forward the email to another recipient, using their email client or webmail service.

Web Browsers

Web browsers are software applications that are used to access and view websites on the internet. They allow users to navigate the World Wide Web (WWW) and view web pages that are hosted on web servers around the world.

Web browsers use a variety of protocols and standards, such as Hypertext Transfer Protocol (HTTP), Hypertext Markup Language (HTML), and Cascading Style Sheets (CSS), to render web pages on the user's screen. They also support other web technologies, such as JavaScript, that allow websites to provide interactivity and dynamic content.

Some popular web browsers include Google Chrome, Mozilla Firefox, Apple Safari, Microsoft Edge, and Opera. Each web browser has its own features and capabilities, such as tabbed browsing, bookmarks, and extensions, that allow users to customize their browsing experience. Web browsers also play an important role in internet security, as they implement various security features, such as SSL/TLS encryption and phishing protection, to protect users from online threats.

Search Engines

Search engines are software applications that are used to search for information on the internet. They allow users to enter keywords or phrases related to the information they are looking for, and then provide a list of relevant websites and other online resources that match their search query.

Some popular search engines include Google, Bing and Yahoo. Each search engine has its own features and capabilities, such as advanced search options, image and video search, and personalized search results based on the user's search history.

Search engines play a critical role in information retrieval on the internet, enabling users to quickly and easily find the information they need. They are used for a wide range of purposes, from research and education to shopping and entertainment.

But how do search engines work? Search engines work by using specialized software programs called spiders or crawlers to systematically browse the web, following links from one web page to another and indexing the content of each page. The algorithms take into account a variety of factors, such as the keywords used on a webpage, the quality and relevance of the content, and the popularity and authority of the website.

Here is a brief overview of how search engines work:

1. Crawling: The search engine's spider starts by crawling a web page, following links to other pages on the same site and to other sites on the web.

2. Indexing: As the spider crawls the web, it collects information about each page it visits, including the page's content, keywords, and other metadata. This information is then stored in a database, which is used to generate search results.

3. Ranking: When a user enters a search query, the search engine uses an algorithm to rank the indexed pages based on their relevance to the query. The algorithm takes into account a variety of factors, such as the keywords used on the page, the quality and relevance of the content, and the popularity and authority of the website.

4. Displaying results: The search engine then displays a list of search results, with the most relevant pages at the top of the list. The user can then click on a search result to visit the corresponding web page.

At some point in time, you might be wondering how search engines earn money? The answer is simple: search engines earn money primarily through advertising and data mining. Here are some of the ways that search engines generate revenue:

1. Paid search advertising: Search engines allow businesses to place ads alongside search results for specific keywords or phrases. These ads are typically sold on a pay-per-click (PPC) basis, meaning that the advertiser only pays when a user clicks on their ad.

2. Display advertising: Search engines may also display banner ads or other types of display ads on their search results pages or on other websites in their advertising network. These ads are typically sold on a cost-per-impression (CPM) basis, meaning that the advertiser pays a fixed amount for every thousand times the ad is displayed.

3. Affiliate marketing: Search engines may earn commissions by promoting products or services through affiliate marketing programs. In this model, the search engine receives a commission for each sale or lead generated through their referral.

4. Data mining: Search engines may also collect and analyze user data to better understand user behavior and

preferences. This data can be used to improve search results, target advertising more effectively, or sell to third-party advertisers.

The Social Media

Social media refers to online platforms and applications that enable users to create, share, and exchange information, ideas, and content with others. Social media allows people to connect and interact with others in real-time, regardless of their location.

Social media platforms are designed to facilitate communication and collaboration among users, allowing them to share text, images, videos, and other types of content. Some popular social media platforms include Facebook, Twitter, Instagram, LinkedIn, and YouTube.

Social media has become an integral part of modern-day communication and has had a significant impact on society, politics, and culture. It has revolutionized the way people connect and communicate with each other, and has enabled the rapid dissemination of information and ideas on a global scale. The historical timeline of social media is as follows:

- 1971: The first email is sent.
- 1978: The first bulletin board system (BBS) is created.
- 1985: America Online (AOL) is founded and becomes one of the first major internet service providers (ISPs).

- 1988: Internet Relay Chat (IRC) is created, allowing users to chat in real-time.
- 1991: The World Wide Web is introduced to the public.
  1994: GeoCities is launched, allowing users to create personal websites.
- 1997: Six Degrees, the first social media platform, is launched.
- 1999: LiveJournal and Blogger are launched, popularizing the concept of blogging.
- 2002: Friendster is launched and becomes one of the first major social media platforms.
- 2003: MySpace is launched and quickly becomes one of the most popular social media platforms.
  2004: Facebook is launched and begins to gain popularity among college students.
- 2005: YouTube is launched, allowing users to share and watch videos online.
- 2006: Twitter is launched, introducing the concept of microblogging.
- 2007: The iPhone is introduced, making social media more accessible on mobile devices.
- 2007: Twitter grew in popularity, with users sending 5,000 tweets per day.
  - Facebook launched its first mobile app for iOS and Android.
  - Tumblr was launched.

- 2008: Facebook surpassed MySpace as the most popular social networking site.
  - Instagram was launched.
  - LinkedIn reached 18 million members.
- 2009: Facebook introduced the Like button.
  - Twitter introduced the hashtag.
  - WhatsApp was launched.
- 2010: Instagram was acquired by Facebook.
  - Pinterest was launched.
  - Google+ was launched.
- 2011: Snapchat was launched.
  - Twitter reached 100 million active users.
  - Google+ reached 90 million users.
- 2012: Facebook reached 1 billion users.
  - Instagram reached 100 million users.
  - LinkedIn reached 200 million members.
- 2013: LinkedIn reached 259 million members.
- 2014: Facebook acquired WhatsApp for $19 billion.
  - Twitter went public.
  - Instagram reached 300 million users.
- 2015: Periscope was launched.
  - Facebook introduced reactions.
  - LinkedIn reached 400 million members.
- 2016: Instagram introduced Stories.
  - Facebook introduced Live video.
  - LinkedIn was acquired by Microsoft for $26.2 billion.

- 2017: Facebook reached 2 billion users.
  - Twitter doubled its character limit to 280.
  - Snapchat went public.
- 2018: Instagram reached 1 billion users.
  - Facebook faced a data privacy scandal.
  - LinkedIn introduced LinkedIn Learning.
- 2019: TikTok became the most downloaded app in the world.
  - Instagram removed likes f in some countries.
  - LinkedIn reached 660 million members.
- 2020: COVID-19 led to increased use of social media.
  - Instagram introduced Reels.
  - Twitter introduced Fleets.

Social Media Uses

Social media is used in various ways in the office and work environment. Some common uses of social media in the workplace include:

1. Marketing and advertising: Many businesses use social media to promote their products and services and to reach a wider audience.

2. Recruiting and hiring: Social media platforms like LinkedIn are often used for recruiting and hiring new employees.

3. Networking: Social media platforms can be used for professional networking, connecting with colleagues and industry professionals, and building relationships.

4. Collaboration and communication: Social media platforms can be used for team collaboration and communication, such as sharing files and information, and conducting virtual meetings.

5. Customer service: Many businesses use social media to provide customer service and support, such as responding to customer inquiries and complaints.

6. Training and development: Social media can be used for training and development purposes, such as providing access to online courses and resources.

7. Employee engagement: Social media can be used to engage employees and build a sense of community within the workplace, such as sharing company news and events, and recognizing employee achievements.

In summary, social media can be a valuable tool for businesses and organizations, but it is important to use it in a responsible and professional manner. Employers should have clear policies and guidelines in place for the use of social media in the workplace, and employees should be aware of the potential risks and consequences of inappropriate social media.

Social media has had a significant impact on our way of life in several ways:

1. Communication: Social media has changed the way we communicate with each other. We can now connect with people from all over the world instantly and easily.

2. Information: Social media has changed the way we access and consume information. We can now access news, entertainment, and educational resources from anywhere at any time.

3. Relationships: Social media has changed the way we build and maintain relationships. We can now connect with friends, family, and acquaintances from all over the world, and maintain those relationships through social media.

4. Business: Social media has changed the way businesses operate. Companies can now connect with customers and promote their products or services through social media.

5. Self-expression: Social media has changed the way we express ourselves. We can now share our thoughts, opinions, and creativity through photos, videos, and other media.

6. Attention span: Social media has changed the way we process information and our attention span. We now have a shorter attention span due to the constant stream of information on social media.

7. Social norms: Social media has changed our social norms and expectations. We now expect instant gratification and constant connection, which can impact our mental health and relationships.

Pro's and Con's

Social media has both positive and negative impacts on us. The pros and cons of social media are:

Pros:

1. Connection: Social media allows people to connect with friends, family, and acquaintances all over the world.

2. Information: Social media provides access to a vast amount of information, including news, entertainment, and educational resources.

3. Business: Social media provides a platform for businesses to connect with customers and promote their products or services.

4. Creativity: Social media provides a platform for people to express themselves creatively through photos, videos, and other media.

5. Awareness: Social media can raise awareness about important issues and promote social justice causes.

Cons:

1. Addiction: Social media can be addictive and lead to excessive use, which can negatively impact mental health and productivity.

2. Cyberbullying: Social media can be used to bully and harass others, which can have serious mental health consequences.

3. Privacy: Social media can compromise privacy and expose personal information to the public.

4. Misinformation: Social media can spread false information and conspiracy theories, which can be harmful to individuals and society.

5. Comparison: Social media can lead to feelings of inadequacy and low self-esteem as people compare themselves to others.

The most popular social media platforms as of 2022 are:

1. Facebook - with over 2.8 billion monthly active users, Facebook is the largest social media platform in the world. It allows users to connect with friends and family, join groups, and share content.

2. YouTube - with over 2 billion monthly active users, YouTube is the largest video-sharing platform in the world. It allows users to upload and watch videos on a wide range of topics.

3. WhatsApp - with over 2 billion monthly active users, WhatsApp is a messaging app that allows users to send messages, make voice and video calls, and share media.

4. Instagram - with over 1.2 billion monthly active users, Instagram is a photo and video-sharing platform that allows users to share their content with followers and connect with others.

5. TikTok - with over 689 million monthly active users, TikTok is a short-form video-sharing app that allows users to create and share videos on a wide range of topics.

6. LinkedIn - with over 740 million registered users, LinkedIn is a professional networking platform that allows users to connect with other professionals, search for jobs, and share content related to their industry.

7. Twitter - with over 353 million monthly active users, Twitter is a microblogging platform that allows users to share short messages, called tweets, with their followers.

8. Snapchat - with over 280 million daily active users, Snapchat is a messaging app that allows users to send disappearing photos and videos, as well as share stories and connect with friends.

Facebook Dominates the Social Media Landscape

Monthly active users of selected social networks and messaging services*

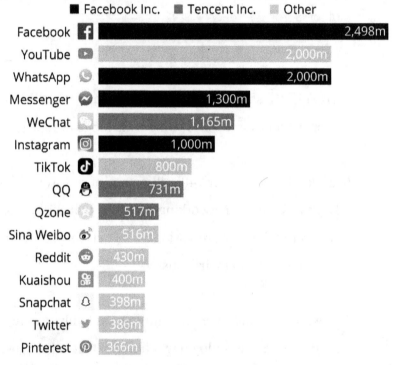

Facebook Inc. ■ Tencent Inc. ■ Other

Facebook	2,498m
YouTube	2,000m
WhatsApp	2,000m
Messenger	1,300m
WeChat	1,165m
Instagram	1,000m
TikTok	800m
QQ	731m
Qzone	517m
Sina Weibo	516m
Reddit	430m
Kuaishou	400m
Snapchat	398m
Twitter	386m
Pinterest	366m

* April 2020 or latest available
Source: Company data via DataReportal Global Digital Statshot

IoT

The Internet of Things (IoT) refers to the network of physical devices, vehicles, home appliances, and other items that are connected to the internet and can communicate with each other. These devices are embedded with sensors, software, and other technologies that allow them to collect and exchange data.

The IoT is based on the concept of connecting everyday objects to the internet, allowing them to be controlled and monitored remotely. This has the potential to revolutionize many industries, including healthcare, transportation, and manufacturing.

Some examples of IoT devices include:

1. Smart home devices, such as thermostats, lighting systems, and security cameras, that can be controlled remotely through a smartphone app.

2. Wearable devices, such as fitness trackers and smartwatches, that can collect and transmit data about a person's health and fitness.

3. Industrial sensors and devices, such as those used in manufacturing and logistics, that can monitor and optimize processes in real-time.

4. Connected vehicles, such as cars and trucks, that can communicate with other vehicles and traffic infrastructure to improve safety and efficiency.

The IoT has the potential to transform the way we live and work, but it also raises concerns about privacy and security. As more devices become connected to the internet, it is important to ensure that they are secure and that users' data is protected.

Discussion Guide

1. Enumerate the five (5) types of Software applications according to their usage. Give an example for each type.

2. What are the advantages and disadvantages of using social media?

3. How does social media impact your life as a student/ professional?

4. Which among the following are considered as search engines:
   a. Google
   b. Chrome
   c. Yahoo
   d. Bing
   e. Oracle

f. Google Search

g. Baidu

Activity Guide

1. Create an account and use the following social media platforms and share your experiences (both positive and negative) to your colleagues:

   o Facebook

   o Twitter

   o Instagram

   o Snapchat

   o Tiktok

   o Youtube

   o Whatsapp

2. Use different search engines and compare your experience on each of them. Which one is better than the other? Why?

Chapter 4: Data Security and Privacy

What is Data Security?

Definition

Data privacy refers to the protection of personal information and data from unauthorized access, use, or disclosure. It involves implementing measures to ensure that personal data is collected, processed, and stored in a secure and confidential manner.

Data privacy is important for individuals, businesses, and organizations that collect and process personal data, such as names, addresses, social security numbers, and financial information.

Data Security Breach

A data security breach is an incident in which sensitive, protected, or confidential data is accessed, viewed, stolen, or used by unauthorized individuals or entities. A data breach can occur due to various reasons, such as a cyberattack, human error, or system glitches. When a data security breach occurs, it is important to take immediate action to contain the breach, investigate the incident, and notify affected individuals. This may involve resetting passwords, implementing additional security measures, and providing identity theft protection services to affected individuals.

When a data breach occurs, the compromised data can be used for fraudulent activities, identity theft, financial loss, and reputational damage. Some common types of data breaches include hacking, malware, phishing, physical theft and inside threats.

Hacking

This involves unauthorized access to a computer system or network to steal sensitive data. Hacking is the unauthorized access, modification, or manipulation of computer systems, networks, or software. It is typically done by individuals or groups with advanced technical skills and knowledge of computer systems and networks.

Hacking can be done for various reasons, including financial gain, political activism, or personal satisfaction. It can result in a range of negative consequences, including data breaches, identity theft, financial loss, and reputational damage.

Some common types of hacking include:

- Malware attacks: This involves the use of malicious software, such as viruses, worms, and Trojans, to gain unauthorized access to a computer system or network.

- Password attacks: This involves the use of brute force or other techniques to guess or crack passwords and gain access to a computer system or network.

- Social engineering: This involves the use of psychological manipulation to trick individuals into providing sensitive information or granting access to computer systems or networks.

- Denial of Service (DoS) attacks: This involves overwhelming a computer system or network with a flood of traffic to make it unavailable to legitimate users.

- Man-in-the-middle attacks: This involves intercepting and altering communications between two parties to gain access to sensitive information.

- Hacking is illegal and can result in serious legal consequences, including fines and imprisonment. It is important to take steps to protect computer systems and networks from hacking, such as implementing strong passwords, using antivirus software, and regularly updating software and security systems.

Misconceptions about hacking. There are several misconceptions about hacking, including:

- Hacking is always illegal: While many types of hacking are illegal, there are some forms of hacking that are legal and ethical. For example, white hat hackers are hired by organizations to test their security systems and identify vulnerabilities.

- Hackers are always criminals: While some hackers engage in criminal activities, such as stealing sensitive data or disrupting computer systems, there are also hackers who use their skills for positive purposes, such as improving computer security or exposing vulnerabilities.

- Hacking is always done for malicious purposes: While some hackers engage in hacking for malicious purposes, such as stealing personal information or disrupting computer systems, there are also hackers who engage in hacking for ethical purposes, such as exposing vulnerabilities or improving computer security.

- Hacking is easy: Hacking requires advanced technical skills and knowledge of computer systems and networks. It is not a simple process and requires a significant amount of time and effort to master.

- Hacking is always done remotely: While some hacking can be done remotely, such as through the use of malware or phishing attacks, there are also forms of hacking that require physical access to a computer system or network.

It is important to have a clear understanding of what hacking is and is not, and to recognize that there are both ethical and unethical forms of hacking.

There are several steps you can take to prevent hacking, including:

1. Use strong and unique passwords: Use strong passwords that are difficult to guess and use a different password for each account.

2. Keep software and security systems up to date: Regularly update your operating system, software, and security systems to ensure that they are protected against the latest threats.

3. Use antivirus software: Use antivirus software to protect your computer from malware and other malicious software.

4. Be wary of suspicious emails and websites: Do not click on links or download attachments from suspicious emails or websites.

5. Use two-factor authentication: Use two-factor authentication to add an extra layer of security to your accounts.

6. Be careful with public Wi-Fi: Avoid using public Wi-Fi for sensitive activities, such as online banking or shopping.

7. Use a virtual private network (VPN): Use a VPN to encrypt your internet connection and protect your online activities from prying eyes.

8. Limit the amount of personal information you share online: Be careful about sharing personal information online, such as your full name, date of birth, and address.

9. Keep backups of important data: Keep backups of important data to protect against data loss in the event of a security breach.

10. Educate yourself about hacking and security: Stay informed about the latest security threats and best practices for protecting your computer and personal information.

In summary , preventing hacking requires a combination of strong security measures, awareness of potential threats, and a commitment to staying informed about the latest security practices.

Malware

This involves the use of malicious software to gain unauthorized access to a computer system or network.

Malware (short for "malicious software") is any type of software that is designed to harm, disrupt, or exploit computer systems, networks, or devices. Malware can take many forms, including viruses, worms, Trojans, spyware, adware, and ransomware.

Malware can be distributed through various methods, including email attachments, infected software downloads, and malicious websites. Once installed on a computer system or network, malware can cause a range of negative consequences, including data breaches, identity theft, financial loss, and reputational damage.Some common types of malware include:

1. Viruses: These are programs that replicate themselves and infect other programs and files on a computer system or network.

2. Worms: These are programs that spread through computer networks and can cause damage to systems and networks.

3. Trojans: These are programs that appear to be legitimate software but contain hidden malicious code.

4. Spyware: This is software that is designed to collect information about a user's online activities without their knowledge or consent.

5. Adware: This is software that displays unwanted advertisements on a user's computer or device.

6. Ransomware: This is software that encrypts a user's files and demands payment in exchange for the decryption key.

In short, malware is a serious threat to computer and network security. It is important to take steps to protect against malware, such as using antivirus software, keeping software and security systems up to date, and being cautious when opening email attachments or downloading software from the internet.

Phishing

This involves the use of fraudulent emails or websites to trick individuals into providing sensitive information. Phishing is a type of cyber attack in which attackers use fraudulent emails, text messages, or websites to trick individuals into providing sensitive information, such as passwords, credit card numbers, or other personal information. The goal of phishing is to steal sensitive information or gain access to computer systems or networks.

Phishing attacks typically involve creating a fake email or website that appears to be from a legitimate source, such as a bank, social media platform, or online retailer. The email or website may ask the user to provide sensitive information, such as a password or credit card number, or may contain a link or attachment that, when clicked, installs malware on the user's computer.

Phishing attacks can be difficult to detect, as they often appear to be from legitimate sources and may use convincing language and graphics. However, there are some common signs of a phishing attack, including:

1. The email or website contains spelling or grammar errors.

2. The email or website asks for sensitive information, such as a password or credit card number.

3. The email or website contains a sense of urgency or threat, such as a warning that the user's account will be suspended if they do not provide information.

4. The email or website contains a suspicious link or attachment.

To protect against phishing attacks, it is important to be cautious when opening emails or clicking on links, especially if they are from unknown sources. It is also important to keep software and security systems up to date, use strong passwords, and enable two-factor authentication whenever possible.

There have been several recent phishing controversies in the Philippines, including:

1. Philippine Red Cross data breach: In October 2020, the Philippine Red Cross announced that it had suffered a data breach that exposed the personal information of over 100,000 blood donors. The breach was caused by a phishing attack that tricked a staff member into providing their login credentials.

2. Landbank phishing scam: In August 2020, the Land Bank of the Philippines warned customers about a phishing scam that used fake emails and websites to trick customers into providing their personal and financial information. The scam targeted customers who were applying for loans or other financial services.

3. Globe Telecom phishing scam: In July 2020, Globe Telecom warned customers about a phishing scam that used fake emails and websites to trick customers into providing their personal information. The scam promised customers a chance to win prizes if they provided their personal information.

4. PhilHealth data breach: In August 2020, the Philippine Health Insurance Corporation (PhilHealth) suffered a data breach that exposed the personal information of millions of Filipinos. The breach was caused by a vulnerability in the agency's website, which was exploited by hackers using phishing and other techniques.

Physical Theft

This involves the theft of physical devices, such as laptops or mobile phones, that contain sensitive data.

A physical theft data breach occurs when a physical device containing sensitive data is stolen or lost, resulting in the unauthorized access to or exposure of the data. This can include theft or loss of laptops, mobile phones, USB drives, or other physical devices that contain sensitive data.

Physical theft data breaches can have serious consequences, as they can result in the theft of personal information, financial loss, and reputational damage. In some cases, physical theft data breaches can also result in regulatory fines and legal action.

To prevent physical theft data breaches, it is important to take steps to secure physical devices that contain sensitive data, such as:

1. Using strong passwords or biometric authentication to secure devices.

2. Encrypting data stored on devices to prevent unauthorized access.

3. Keeping devices with sensitive data in secure locations when not in use.

4. Regularly backing up important data to prevent data loss in the event of theft or loss.

5. Implementing remote wipe capabilities to erase data from lost or stolen devices.

6. Educating employees on the importance of physical security and how to prevent physical theft data breaches.

Insider Threats

This involves the intentional or unintentional disclosure of sensitive data by individuals within an organization.

An insider threat data breach occurs when a person within an organization, such as an employee or contractor, intentionally or unintentionally causes a data breach by accessing, stealing, or sharing sensitive information. Insider threats can be malicious, such as when an employee steals sensitive data for personal gain or to harm the organization, or they can be accidental, such as when an employee unintentionally exposes sensitive data through a mistake or oversight.

Insider threat data breaches can have serious consequences, as they can result in the theft of sensitive information, financial loss, and reputational damage. In some cases, insider threat data breaches can also result in regulatory fines and legal action.

To prevent insider threat data breaches, it is important to take steps to protect sensitive data and monitor employee activities, such as:

1. Implementing access controls to limit access to sensitive data to authorized personnel.

2. Monitoring employee activities and network traffic to detect potential threats.

3. Educating employees on the importance of data security and the risks of insider threats.

4. Conducting background checks and security screenings for employees and contractors.

5. Implementing data loss prevention (DLP) software to monitor and prevent the unauthorized transfer of sensitive data.

6. Regularly reviewing and updating security policies and procedures.

Reflection / Example

One example of a data breach in a movie is in the film "Ocean's Eleven" (2001). In the movie, a team of thieves plan to rob three Las Vegas casinos by hacking into the security systems and stealing millions of dollars. The team uses a variety of methods to breach the security systems, including using a fake security van to enter the casino, hacking into the surveillance cameras, and using a fake earthquake to disable the power grid. Once they gain access to the vaults, they use explosives to open the

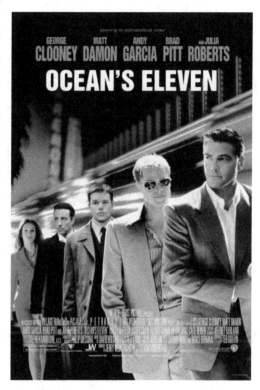

doors and steal the money. While the movie portrays the data breach as a clever heist, it is important to remember that in real life, data breaches can have serious consequences and are illegal.

The Philippine Data Privacy Act

The Philippine Data Privacy Act of 2012 (Republic Act No. 10173) is a law that aims to protect the privacy of personal information in the Philippines. The law was enacted on August 15, 2012, and took effect on September 8, 2012.

The Data Privacy Act establishes the National Privacy Commission (NPC) as the agency responsible for enforcing the law and protecting the privacy of personal information. The law requires organizations to comply with certain data privacy principles, including:

1. Transparency: Organizations must inform individuals about the collection, use, and processing of their personal information.

2. Legitimate purpose: Organizations must collect and process personal information only for legitimate purposes.

3. Proportionality: Organizations must collect and process personal information only to the extent necessary to achieve their legitimate purposes.

4. Data subject participation: Individuals have the right to access, correct, and dispute the accuracy of their personal information.

5. Security: Organizations must implement appropriate security measures to protect personal information against unauthorized access, use, or disclosure.

6. Accountability: Organizations are accountable for complying with the Data Privacy Act and must implement policies and procedures to ensure compliance.

The Data Privacy Act applies to both public and private organizations that collect, use, or process personal information in the Philippines. The law imposes penalties for non-compliance, including fines and imprisonment. To sum it, the Data Privacy Act is an important law that helps protect the privacy of personal information in the Philippines and promotes responsible data handling practices by organizations.

Data Security and Privacy in Social Media

The security of data in social media depends on several factors, including the privacy policies and security measures implemented by social media platforms, the behavior of users on social media, and the potential for cyber attacks and data breaches.

Social media platforms typically collect a large amount of personal information from users, including names, email addresses, birthdates, and other sensitive data. They also collect data on users' activities on the platform, such as the pages they visit and the content they interact with. This data can be used for targeted advertising and other purposes, and it is important for social media platforms to implement strong privacy policies and security measures to protect this data.

Social media platforms typically use encryption to protect user data, but there is still potential for data breaches and cyber attacks. For example, in 2018, Facebook suffered a major data breach that exposed the personal information of millions of users. This breach was caused by a vulnerability in Facebook's code that allowed hackers to gain access to user accounts.

In addition to the security measures implemented by social media platforms, users also play a role in the security of their data. It is important for users to use strong passwords, enable two-factor authentication, and be cautious when sharing personal information on social media. There are several data security risks associated with social media, including:

1. Data breaches: Social media platforms store a large amount of personal information, including names, email addresses, and birthdates. If this information is breached, it can be used for identity theft, financial fraud, and other malicious activities.

2. Malware attacks: Malware can be spread through social media platforms, often through malicious links or attachments. Once installed on a user's device, malware can steal personal information and cause other damage.

3. Phishing attacks: Social media platforms can be used to launch phishing attacks, which trick users into providing their personal information. Phishing attacks can be difficult to detect, as they often appear to be from trusted sources.

4. Social engineering attacks: Social media platforms can be used to gather personal information about users, which can be used to launch social engineering attacks. Social engineering attacks use

psychological manipulation to trick users into providing sensitive information or granting access to computer systems or networks.

5. Cyberbullying: Social media platforms can be used for cyberbullying, which can cause emotional distress and reputational damage. Cyberbullying can also escalate into more serious forms of harassment and abuse.

Steps in Preventing Personal Data Risks in using Social Media.

To ensure personal data security when using social media, you can take the following steps:

1. Use strong and unique passwords: Use strong passwords that are difficult to guess and use a different password for each social media account.

2. Enable two-factor authentication: Two-factor authentication adds an extra layer of security to your social media accounts by requiring a code sent to your phone or email in addition to your password.

3. Be cautious about what you share: Be careful about the personal information you share on social media, such

as your full name, date of birth, and address. Avoid sharing sensitive information, such as your social security number or financial information.

4. Adjust your privacy settings: Review and adjust your privacy settings on social media to limit who can see your posts and personal information.

5. Be wary of suspicious links and messages: Do not click on links or download attachments from suspicious messages or posts on social media.

6. Keep your software and security systems up to date: Regularly update your operating system, software, and security systems to ensure that they are protected against the latest threats.

7. Use anti-virus software: Use anti-virus software to protect your computer from malware and other malicious software.

8. Avoid public Wi-Fi: Avoid using public Wi-Fi for sensitive activities, such as logging into your social media accounts.

9. Educate yourself about social media security: Stay informed about the latest security threats and best practices for social media security.

Cyberbullying

Cyberbullying is the use of technology, such as social media, text messages, or email, to harass, intimidate, or humiliate someone. Cyberbullying can take many forms, including sending threatening or abusive messages, spreading rumors or lies about someone online, or posting embarrassing photos or videos of someone without their consent.

Cyberbullying can have serious consequences for the victim, including emotional distress, depression, anxiety, and even suicide. It can also have long-lasting effects on the victim's reputation and relationships.

Cyberbullying can be difficult to detect and prevent, as it often takes place online and can be anonymous. However, there are steps that can be taken to prevent and address cyberbullying, including:

1. Educating children and teenagers about the dangers of cyberbullying and how to stay safe online.

2. Encouraging open communication between parents, teachers, and children about cyberbullying.

3. Monitoring children's online activities and social media use.

4. Teaching children to be respectful and kind online, and to report any incidents of cyberbullying to a trusted adult.

5. Encouraging social media platforms and internet service providers to take a more proactive role in preventing cyberbullying.

In the Philippines, cyberbullying is considered a criminal offense under the Cybercrime Prevention Act of 2012 (Republic Act No. 10175). The law defines cyberbullying as the use of any form of technology to harass, intimidate, or bully another person.

The legal consequences of cyberbullying in the Philippines can include fines and imprisonment. Under the Cybercrime Prevention Act, cyberbullying is punishable by imprisonment of up to six months, or a fine of up to 200,000 Philippine pesos, or both.

In addition to the legal consequences, cyberbullying can also have other consequences, such as damage to the victim's reputation and emotional distress. Victims of cyberbullying may also be entitled to civil damages, such as compensation for medical expenses or lost income. Schools, parents, and law enforcement agencies all have a role to play in preventing and addressing cyberbullying, and it is important to work together to create a  safe and supportive environment for all.

The Department of Education (DepEd) recorded more than 260,000 cases of physical bullying in school in just one school year. According to a "24 Oras" report by Bernadette Reyes, a total of 264,668 cases of physical bullying were reported in the 2021-2022 school year.

There are also 7,758 cases of cyberbullying, 7,800 cases of gender-based bullying and 17,258 cases of social bullying.

Despite the alarming number, many cases probably went unreported. DepEd launched its hotline for students to report abuse and a program that focuses on student mental health.

Cyberlibel

Cyberlibel in the Philippines refers to the act of committing libel through the use of the internet or other forms of electronic communication, such as social media, email, or text messages. Libel is a criminal offense under Philippine law, and it is defined as the publication of a false statement that is intended to harm the reputation of another person.

The Cybercrime Prevention Act of 2012 (Republic Act No. 10175) includes provisions that address cyberlibel. Under the law, cyberlibel is punishable by imprisonment and fines. The penalties for cyberlibel are more severe than those for traditional libel, and the law has been criticized for potentially infringing on freedom of speech and the press.

In 2012, the Cybercrime Prevention Act was challenged in the Philippine Supreme Court, and several provisions, including those related to cyberlibel, were declared constitutional. However, the law continues to be the subject of debate and controversy in the Philippines.

To be considered cyberlibel, the false statement must be published online or through electronic communication, and it must be intended to harm the reputation of another person. The statement must also be false and must be made with knowledge of its falsity or with reckless disregard for its truth or falsity.

In the Philippines, victims of cyber libel may file a criminal complaint against the person who made the false statement. If found guilty, the person may be sentenced to imprisonment and fines. Victims may also be entitled to civil damages, such as compensation for the harm caused to their reputation.

Discussion Guide

1. What is Republic Act 10173? What are the responsibilities of institutions and offices as per specified under the law?
2. What is Republic Act No. 10175? What are considered as crimes under the law? What are the penalties for each of the acts prohibited under the law?
3. What are the common misconceptions of hacking?
4. As a privacy officer or IT specialist, how will you prevent data security breaches?

Activity Guide

1. Do you have any experience in cyberbullying? Ask around your colleagues and friends if they have similar experiences.

How did they cope up with such an experience? What legal actions did they take?

2. Seek an audience with your school or office head. Ask for a copy of your institution's Data Protection Policy if any. If there is none, draft one and submit for possible approval.

3. Check your Facebook's Security and Privacy settings particularly:

   a. Who can access to your profile
   b. Who can track your activities in the internet such as shopping or search trends
   c. Who can track your locations
   d. What apps have access to your information
   e. Who can view and comment on your posts

4. Check your browser's preference/ settings. Check whether or not your passwords are autosaved/ cached.

Bibliography

Amies, A. (2012). *Developing and Hosting Applications on the Cloud*. IBM Press.

Bridle, James (2019). *New dark age: technology and the end of the future*. Verso.

Donham, P. (2018). *Introduction to Computer Science (First Edition)*. Cognella Academic Publishing.

Herrera, C., & Hajek, D. (2019). *Introduction to Computers, 2019 Edition*. Independently Published.

History of the Computer timeline | Timetoast timelines. Retrieved September 21, 2023, from https://www.timetoast.com/timelines/

Burks, A. R., & Burks, A. W. (1988). *The First Electronic Computer*. University of Michigan Press.

Computer Architecture. (2016). CRC Press.

Deitel, H. M. (1990). *An Introduction to Operating Systems*. Addison Wesley Publishing Company.

DepEd logs over 260K cases of physical bullying in SY 2021-2022 . Retrieved September 21, 2023, from https://gmanetwork.com/ news/topstories/nation/

Donald Eadie (1968). *Introduction to the Basic Computer*. Prentice-Hall.

Introduction to Operating Systems. Retrieved September 21, 2023, from http://cis2.oc.ctc.edu/oc_apps/Westlund/

Joshi, K., & Rutledge, P.-A. (2011). *Using Facebook*. Pearson Education.

Learning, E. E. (2015). *Introduction to Computers and Information Technology*. Pearson.

OpenAI. (2023). *AI ChatBot*. (Version 2.3)

O'Regan, G. (2012). *A Brief History of Computing*. Springer Science & Business Media.

Ronald J. Leach (27 January 2016). *Introduction to Software Engineering*. CRC Press. ISBN 978-1-4987-0528-8.

Silberschatz, A., Galvin, P. B., & Gagne, G. (2014). *Operating System Concepts*.

Shelly, G. B., Freund, S. M., & Vermaat, M. E. (2010). *Introduction to Computers*. Cengage Learning.

Wang, M. (2020). Key Concepts of Computer Studies. BCcampus. https://opentextbc.ca/computerstudies/

Wempen, F. (2014). *Computing Fundamentals*. John Wiley & Sons.

Zuse, K. (2013). *The Computer - My Life*. Springer Science & Business Media.

Photo Sources:

- *Photo by Zane Lee on Unsplash*
- *Photo Retrieved from https://medium.com/@VijayBala_*
- *Photo retrieved from https://www.nvisia.com/*
- *Photo from https://www.linkedin.com*
- *Photo by ZHENYU LUO on Unsplash*
- *Photo by Owen Beard on Unsplash*
- *Photo by Lars Kienle on Unsplash*
- *Photo from https://www.linkedin.com/pulse/understanding-domain-*
- *Photo from https://medium.com*
- *Photo from https://moosend.com/*
- *Photo by John Salvino on Unsplash*
- *Photo by Philbo ▬ on Unsplash*
- *Photo by Georgie Cobbs on Unsplash*
- *Photo from https://techandlaws.com/*
- *Photo from https://www.projectline.ca*

About the Author

 Prof. Paul Omar P. Gangoso is a U.S. Professional and Academic Exchange Fellow. With degrees in Information Technology, Multimedia Arts and Literature, he has a Master's Degree in Public Management, and a Master's Degree in Information Technology and PhD in IT. He is also a TESDA-certified Trainer and Assessor in Photography NC II, Visual Graphics Design NC III, 2D Animation NC II, 3D Animation NC III, Computer Systems NC II, Film Production NTR and 12 other qualifications.

Prof. Gangoso is currently serving as the Administrator/ CEO of the Pagadian City Chamber School and the Board Chairman of the Southeast Asian Institute of Public Management Group of Companies.

www.ingramcontent.com/pod-product-compliance
Lightning Source LLC
LaVergne TN
LVHW051333050326
832903LV00031B/3519